Inclusive Growth in Seoul, Korea

Please cite this publication as:
OECD (2018), *Inclusive Growth in Seoul, Korea*, OECD Publishing, Paris.
http://dx.doi.org/10.1787/9789264290198-en

ISBN 978-92-64-29018-1 (print)
ISBN 978-92-64-29019-8 (PDF)

Photo credits: Cover @GettyImages

Corrigenda to OECD publications may be found on line at: *www.oecd.org/about/publishing/corrigenda.htm*.

Foreword

In the face of rising inequalities in cities, many mayors from around the world have taken a stand. The OECD launched the Champion Mayors for Inclusive Growth initiative in March 2016 as part of the OECD Inclusive Growth initiative, bringing together nearly 50 local leaders from around the world who have made the fight against inequalities a central policy priority. Since its inception, this global coalition, which draws mayors from Paris to New York, from Cape Town to Medellín, from Los Angeles to Seoul, has delivered three major political outcomes, including the *New York Proposal*, the *Paris Action Plan*, and the *Seoul Implementation Agenda*. These documents reflect the shared commitment of mayors to work together to advance more inclusive cities.

This report, *Inclusive Growth in Seoul, Korea,* is the first OECD study to assess the performance of a city along a range of inclusive growth dimensions. It builds on a wealth of OECD research and data around inclusive growth and well-being, in particular OECD (2016), *Making Cities Work for All: Data and Actions for Inclusive Growth* and OECD (2014), *How's Life in Your Region?*

This analysis of inclusive growth in Seoul goes beyond income inequality to assess the barriers faced by specific groups and geographic areas in the city. It addresses trends and challenges across four key dimensions, building on the pillars of the *New York Proposal* and the *Paris Action Plan*: education, labour market, housing and the urban environment, and infrastructure and public services. It also delves deeper into two major policy efforts by Seoul Metropolitan Government, which reflect common challenges facing many local governments to advance inclusive growth: how can local authorities ensure that strategies to address climate change *also* protect and benefit the most vulnerable populations; and how can city authorities help level the playing field for small firms and entrepreneurs?

While local authorities make critical contributions to delivering inclusive growth for their citizens, the fundamental role of national policies and an enabling environment cannot be understated. This study also identifies strengths and gaps within the national policy environment in Korea that can either help or hinder Seoul's efforts towards inclusive growth.

This series of case studies is designed to support leaders and policy makers in both national and local governments in tackling one of the most pernicious policy challenges of our time: rising inequalities.

Acknowledgements

This report, *Inclusive Growth in Seoul, Korea,* was developed as part of the Champion Mayors for Inclusive Growth initiative, which is a major pillar of the OECD Inclusive Growth initiative, led by Gabriela Ramos, OECD Chief of Staff and Sherpa to the G20, and coordinated by Romina Boarini in the Office of the Secretary-General.

The study was produced by the OECD Centre for Entrepreneurship, SMEs, Regions and Cities (CFE), led by Lamia Kamal-Chaoui, Director, who oversees the Champion Mayors initiative, and coordinated by Marissa Plouin, Coordinator of the OECD Champion Mayors initiative. For more information about this initiative, please visit www.oecd-inclusive.com/champion-mayors.

The Secretariat would like to thank the Seoul Metropolitan Government (SMG), led by Mayor Wonsoon Park. In particular, sincere thanks are due to Dongruk Suh, Deputy Mayor of Economic Planning; Taehee Kim, Director of Economic Policy Division; and the Inclusive Growth team, including Kiwoong Lee, Sanghun Ku and Nayeon Kim, for their excellent and sustained collaboration throughout the process. The Secretariat also wishes to acknowledge the many experts and policy makers who participated in the OECD study mission in June 2017, including representatives from Seoul Metropolitan Government (Economic Planning; Climate Change and Sustainability; City Transportation; Urban Regeneration; Water Circulation Safety; Employment and Labour); Seoul Business Agency; Seoul Social Economy Centre; the Seoul Social Economy Network; Global Platform for Promoting Social Economy (GSEF); Seoul Energy Dream Centre; Seoul Energy Corporation; Seoul Credit Guarantee Foundation; Korea Federation of SMEs (KBIZ); Korea Chamber of Commerce and Industry; and experts from the Seoul Institute.

The study has benefitted from contributions from OECD experts from CFE and the Environment Directorate (ENV). Chapter 1 was drafted by Oscar Huerta Melchor and Andres Sanabria (CFE); Chapter 2 was drafted by Virginie Marchal (ENV); and Chapter 3 was drafted by Sandra Hannig (CFE), with inputs from external expert Declan Carroll. Sena Segbedzi, Kate Brooks and Hyung-Tae Kim (CFE) provided valuable research assistance and editorial support.

Special thanks are also due to the City of Paris, and in particular, Faustine Bidaud, Project officer, Climate and Innovation in the General Direction for International Relations, who served as a Peer Reviewer for this study.

The report benefitted from valuable comments from colleagues, including during the initial brainstorming phase around the alignment of climate change and inclusive growth strategies, from CFE: Lamia Kamal-Chaoui, Joaquim Oliveira Martins, Rudiger Ahrend, Sylvain Giguère, Jon Potter, Soo-Jin Kim, Debra Mountford, Paolo Veneri, Jonathan Barr and Eric Gonnard; from ENV: Simon Buckle, Walid Oueslati, Xavier Leflaive, Michael Mullan, Jennifer Calder, Jaco Tavanier and Shaun Reidy; and from the Office of the Secretary-General: Romina Boarini. The study was presented and approved by the LEED Directing Committee, and also presented at the Working Party on Urban Policy and the Working Party on Climate, Investment and Development.

Barbara Cachova (CFE) provided logistical support. Pauline Arbel (CFE) designed the cover. Cicely Dupont-Nivore and Pilar Philip (CFE) prepared the report for publication.

Table of contents

Tables

Figures

Boxes

Abbreviations and acronyms

B2B	Business-to-Business
BDS	Business Development Services
BERD	Business enterprise Expenditure on Research and Development
BOK	Bank of Korea
BRP	Building Retrofit Programme
CES	Croatian Employment Service
EDA	Economic Democratisation Agenda
ETS	Emission Trading Scheme
EU	European Union
GDP	Gross Domestic Product
GEM	Global Entrepreneurship Monitoring
GHG	Greenhouse Gas
KPI	Key Performance Indicator
LEDS	Low-emission Development Strategies
LEZ	Low Emission Zone
LPG	Liquefied petroleum gas
MFP	Multifactor Productivity
NEET	Neither Employed nor in Education or Training
NYC	New York City
PISA	Programme for International Student Assessment
$PM_{2.5}$	Fine Particulate Matter with a diameter of less than 2.5 micrometres
PM_{10}	Fine Particulate Matter with a diameter of less than 10 micrometres
PMR	Product Market Regulation
SDG	Sustainable Development Goal
SMBA	Small and Medium Business Administration
SME	Small and Medium-sized Enterprise
SMG	Seoul Metropolitan Government
STEM	Science, Technology, Engineering, and Mathematics
STI	Science, Technology and Innovation
TEA	Total Early-Stage Entrepreneurial Activity

TL2	Territorial Level 2 region
TOD	Transport-oriented Development
TOE	Tons of oil equivalent
WHO	World Health Organization

Executive summary

Echoing broader trends in Korea, Seoul's rapid economic development and urbanisation in recent decades has generated significant prosperity, but economic growth has not been equally distributed across territories and populations. Income inequalities in Korea are the seventh-highest in the OECD, and regional disparities are also relatively high and have been on the rise over the past decade.

Quality public services are the foundation for inclusive growth in Seoul, yet some groups face challenges

Seoul offers its 10 million inhabitants – 25 million within the broader metropolitan area – high quality public services, including education, health and public transport. These services help provide a strong foundation for inclusive growth to all residents, regardless of their income levels or geography within the city. However, a number of pressing challenges remain, particularly for certain social groups. The city faces a rapid and massive demographic transition, with a fast-ageing population, nearly half of whom are living below the poverty line. In addition, a rigid labour market – a key feature of the Korean economy more broadly – divides workers into two groups, regular and non-regular workers; non-regular workers have fixed-term contracts and weaker social protections, and earn around 64% of the hourly wage of regular workers. Women, youth, seniors and migrants face additional hurdles in the labour market: women are paid 63% of men's average wage – the highest gender pay gap in the OECD, while labour market inactivity rates among youth are among the highest in the OECD. These challenges point to critical barriers for specific groups to fully participate in the city's economy.

Seoul is pioneering efforts to put citizen welfare and inclusion at the core of climate strategies

A changing climate risks exacerbating existing inequalities and disadvantages in Seoul. Climate change damages, which are expected to escalate in Seoul, are likely to disproportionately affect already economically vulnerable groups, who are either more vulnerable to health impacts or lack insurance and social safety nets to help them recover from damages. Vulnerable groups in Seoul include non-regular workers, low-income households as well as those with lower levels of education, women and the elderly. For instance, between 2000 and 2010, mortality rates increased by 8.4% during heat waves, with higher risks recorded for women versus men, older versus younger residents, and those with no education versus some education.

Against a backdrop of strong national policy framework for climate change action and green growth, Seoul Metropolitan Government (SMG) has been at the forefront of city efforts to put citizen welfare and participation at the core of its ambitious climate change strategies. In particular, SMG has been effective in linking energy-efficiency measures with those to address energy poverty: this is especially relevant in Seoul, where one in ten households faces energy poverty. Through the *Promise of Seoul* initiative, SMG introduced a comprehensive plan to address climate change mitigation, adaptation and citizen welfare in a mutually reinforcing way, while engaging citizens at all stages of the policy making process. Indeed, citizen participation is an essential part of the implementation of a number of SMG initiatives, such as the *Energy Welfare Public-Private Partnership Programme* and *Energy Self-sufficient Communities,* which are designed to deliver emissions reduction while raising awareness and boosting solidarity.

Nonetheless, several dimensions of the city's already impressive efforts could be strengthened. First, SMG could consider collecting data and developing indicators to understand the interactions of climate and inclusive growth outcomes, within and beyond the city's administrative boundaries. Second, SMG could mainstream climate and inclusive growth objectives in transport, land-use and urban planning policy making; much of the city's efforts thus far have centred on the energy sector, while other important policy areas present opportunities for action. Third, SMG could develop a long-term low-emission development strategy at the city level; such strategies can be an important policy tool to place short-term actions in the context of the long-term structural changes required to transition to a low-carbon, resilient economy by 2050. Finally, SMG could take measures to overcome administrative fragmentation within the city administration to break down policy siloes. At higher levels of government, more needs to be done to align policies with inclusive growth and environmental objectives; the labour market and energy sector in particular require considerable reforms at national level.

SMEs and entrepreneurship are a crucial vector for inclusive growth in Seoul

Small and medium-sized enterprises (SMEs) help drive inclusive growth in Seoul. Micro and small firms represent about 98% of the business population and account for nearly 60% of employment in Seoul, providing income and jobs for a large share of the population. However, they face a number of challenges. The gap between SMEs and large firm productivity in Korea is the largest in the OECD; this can be partially explained by very low levels of innovation and regulatory barriers to entrepreneurship. On top of that, many groups with lower labour market activity rates (women, youth, migrants) are strongly affected by the country's labour market dualism, both in terms of worker status (regular versus non-regular workers) and by firm size (SMEs versus large conglomerates). Many non-regular workers, for instance, work in SMEs. The challenges faced by SMEs and entrepreneurs are universal across Korea, signalling a need for broader national reforms.

In 2016, SMG introduced the *Economic Democratisation Agenda* (EDA), which aims to reduce economic inequality and provide equal opportunity for all citizens to engage in sustainable economic activities. The EDA includes 23 measures divided into 3 categories: partnership, fairness and labour, including measures to support SMEs and entrepreneurs, as well as labour market measures, such as social insurance support to small business owners and the conversion of non-regular working contracts into regular contracts for some public-sector workers. The EDA is effective in identifying many important challenges facing SMEs and disadvantaged groups – notably women, youth and seniors, but will not alone suffice in resolving these challenges. Indeed, part of the stated aim of the EDA is to bring attention to challenges facing SMEs, entrepreneurs and other vulnerable workers in order to spur action at national level.

Several aspects of the EDA could be strengthened. First, SMG could complement the EDA with measures that go beyond protecting SMEs from structural faults of the company, to those that strengthen their productivity and innovation capacity; such measures would be essential to truly level the playing field for firms of all sizes. This includes building a strong ecosystem for inclusive entrepreneurship that ensures access to finance, knowledge and technology. Second, SMG could strengthen monitoring and evaluation to measure the efficiency and impact of different policy measures of the EDA. Finally, SMG could do more to address labour market duality and strengthen entrepreneurship. This includes investments in skills and better access to networks, which is especially important for economically disadvantaged groups that may not have access to the same business connections.

Chapter 1

Inclusive Growth trends and challenges in Seoul

This chapter examines the state of inequalities and inclusive growth in Seoul. It assesses major economic and demographic trends in the Seoul metropolitan area relative to other Korean cities and OECD metropolitan areas. It analyses the challenges facing Seoul inhabitants along four inclusive growth pillars (education; labour markets; housing and the urban environment; infrastructure and public services), focusing on the extent to which certain social groups or inhabitants of specific neighbourhoods face difficulties in fully benefitting from the city's economic and social opportunities.

1.1. Inequalities as a pressing policy challenge in Seoul

Seoul has been at the centre of Korea's political, economic, and social transformation over the past decades. The country has shifted to democracy, experienced rapid urban and economic growth, and achieved high education attainment levels and a technology boom, transitioning into a major global player. Today the city of Seoul, home to one in five Koreans, is the engine of national growth and an economic powerhouse in Asia. Despite a slowdown in recent years, economic growth in the Seoul metropolitan area is still well above the OECD average and that of other major metro areas, such as London, New York and Tokyo.

Despite these achievements, the benefits of economic growth and urbanisation have not been equally distributed. Echoing trends of a growing gap between the rich and the poor across OECD countries (Box 1.1), Korea registers the seventh-highest income gap and the eighth-highest relative poverty rate in the OECD (OECD, 2016a). There are also significant inter-regional income disparities within Korea: Korea recorded the seventh-highest rate of regional disparities among OECD countries in 2013 (OECD, 2016b). With 25.3 million inhabitants, the broader metropolitan area of Seoul, which includes the province of Gyeonggi and Incheon Metropolitan City, concentrates around half of the country's people, firms, employment, and national Gross Domestic Product (GDP).

But inequalities are not just about income, and some demographic groups in Seoul face significant barriers to access social and economic opportunities, including quality housing, transport, education and quality jobs. While Seoul performs relatively well in terms of educational outcomes and access to services, important challenges remain, especially for youth, women, the elderly and migrants. Some of these groups will moreover be more vulnerable to the impacts of a changing climate in Seoul. In addition, there are a number of challenges facing firms – particularly small firms – and individuals in the labour market.

This report, *Inclusive Growth in Seoul, Korea,* assesses Seoul Metropolitan Government's progress towards more Inclusive Growth.

- ***Chapter 1*** examines major urban and economic trends in Seoul, with a special focus on challenges facing vulnerable groups, and assesses a selection of outcomes along the four pillars of the *New York Proposal* and the *Paris Action Plan*: education, labour market, urban environment, and infrastructure and public services.
- ***Chapter 2*** takes a closer look at the impact of climate change on economically vulnerable populations in Seoul, and at the Seoul Metropolitan Government's efforts to bridge strategies for climate change and inclusive growth, building on the *Promise of Seoul,* the city's long-term strategy released in 2015 to achieve an inclusive, low-carbon future.
- ***Chapter 3*** focuses on the city's efforts to level the playing field for small and medium-sized enterprises (SMEs) and provide support to specific populations and economic sectors through its *Economic Democratisation Agenda*.

This report uses three geographical units of analysis: the Capital Region, Seoul metropolitan area, and Seoul City (Figure 1.1):

- When data is not available at a more granular scale, the report will present information at the level of the **Capital Region**. The Capital Region represents the first administrative tier of subnational government in Korea, classified by OECD as a territorial level 2 region (TL2), and is comprised of the city of Seoul as well as the surrounding province of Gyeonggi and Incheon Metropolitan City. The Capital Region was home to a population of 25.3 million in 2016.
- For international comparisons with 291 metropolitan areas in the OECD, data at the level of Seoul's metropolitan area (hereinafter referred as **Seoul metropolitan area**) will be used, consistent with the OECD-European Union (EU) functional urban area definition. The Seoul metropolitan area has a population of 25 million and includes municipalities from the surrounding provinces of Gyeonggi and Incheon.[1]
- Finally, where available, data will be presented for **Seoul city**, which corresponds to the administrative boundaries and policy authority of the Seoul Metropolitan Government (SMG). Seoul city has a population of over 10 million and is divided into 25 districts (*gu*), covering a land area of 605 km², which corresponds to roughly 40% of the population and 13% of the land area of Seoul metropolitan area.

Box 1.1. Inclusive Growth in cities and the global coalition of Champion Mayors at the OECD

Across the OECD, the average income of the richest 10% of the population has grown from seven to ten times that of the poorest 10% in a single generation. But inequalities are not just about money: they affect every dimension of people's lives and well-being, such as life expectancy, education outcomes, and job prospects.

In 2012, the OECD launched the Inclusive Growth initiative as a response to a widening gap between the rich and the poor. The OECD defines Inclusive Growth as "growth that creates opportunities for all segments of the population to participate in the economy and distributes the dividends of increased prosperity fairly across society" (OECD, 2014a). The OECD takes a multidimensional approach, going beyond income to take into account a range of well-being outcomes and policy domains.

Inequalities can be even more acute in cities. According to OECD evidence:

- Income inequality tends to be higher in cities relative to their respective countries (in 10 out of 11 OECD countries surveyed). This is because cities have a wider polarisation of high and low skills and top earners capture a higher share of total income (OECD 2016a).
- Income inequality tends to be higher in larger cities.
- Inequality goes beyond income, affecting every dimension of an individual's life, such as employment opportunities, health and education outcomes. For instance, in London (United Kingdom) and Baltimore (United States), life expectancy can vary by 20 years across neighbourhoods.
- Moreover, income inequality has a clear spatial dimension, with the persistence of neighbourhoods of concentrated wealth and poverty. OECD research found that the most income segregated cities in the Netherlands and France are at comparable levels to the least segregated cities in the United States.
- Even within the same country, income segregation can vary across cities depending on region-specific factors such as labour productivity, the degree of spatial decentralisation, and demography as well as the level of wealth (OECD, 2017a)

In recognition of the key role of cities in tackling inequalities, the OECD created a global coalition of Champion Mayors for Inclusive Growth in March 2016. Together, Champion Mayors delivered the *New York Proposal for Inclusive Growth in Cities* and the *Paris Action Plan for Inclusive Growth in Cities*, which outlined a series of commitments and policy priorities, along four main pillars: 1) Education; 2) Labour markets; 3) Housing and the urban environment; and 4) Infrastructure and public services. These dimensions will serve as a framework to assess Inclusive Growth outcomes beyond income at the city level in this study of Seoul.

This report assesses inequalities and inclusion both in terms of specific geographic areas within Seoul (e.g. whether some neighbourhoods may face more acute challenges relative to others), as well as the impact of policies on specific socio-economic groups (e.g. economically vulnerable groups, such as low income people, women, elderly, children, minorities and migrants).

Source: OECD (2014a); OECD (2016a); OECD (2016c); OECD (2016d); OECD (2017a).

Figure 1.1. Seoul Metropolitan Area (OECD-EU functional urban area) and Seoul city

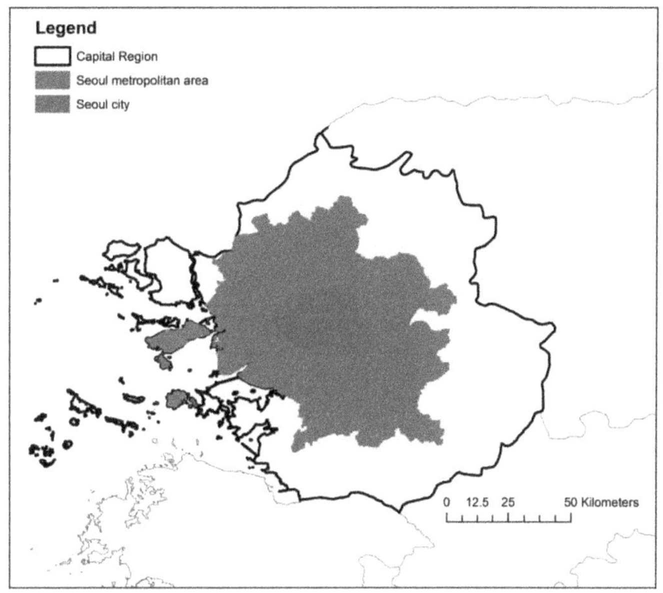

Note: This document and any map included herein are without prejudice to the status of or sovereignty over any territory, to the delimitation of international frontiers and boundaries and to the name of any territory, city or area.
Source: OECD (2017) Metropolitan areas (database) http://dx.doi.org/10.1787/data-00531-en; Global Administrative Areas (GADM) database and Seoul Metropolitan Government.

1.2. Seoul is an economic powerhouse, yet must overcome major demographic challenges

1.2.1. The economic, cultural and political centre of Korea

Economic activity is concentrated in Seoul metropolitan area, which accounts for almost 47% of Korea's firms, 50% of national employment, and 46% of the national GDP. Seoul city alone concentrates more than half of all the companies in the country in the information, communication and financial sectors. Seoul is a hub for large international firms, such as Samsung and LG, and performs gateway functions for the national economy with its logistics platform and world-class Incheon International Airport – the fifth largest in the world in terms of freight traffic (ACI, 2016).

Despite the economic slowdown of the last decade, economic growth in the Seoul metropolitan area is still among the highest across OECD metro areas. The Seoul metropolitan area experienced average GDP growth of 4% between 2000 and 2013, which is above the OECD average (2%) and well above that of other large metro areas such as London (2.2%), New York (1.4%) and Tokyo (1.2%). With roughly half of the country's population, Seoul metropolitan area enjoys the benefits of urbanisation, as high urban densities can reduce transaction costs, make public spending on infrastructure and services more economically viable, and facilitate the generation and diffusion of knowledge, all of which are important factors of growth.

The Capital Region, which includes Seoul, Incheon and Gyeonggi, is the economic leader of the country. Aspects such as the investment in research and development, the share of

Regional performance in selected indicators (as a share of the country average)

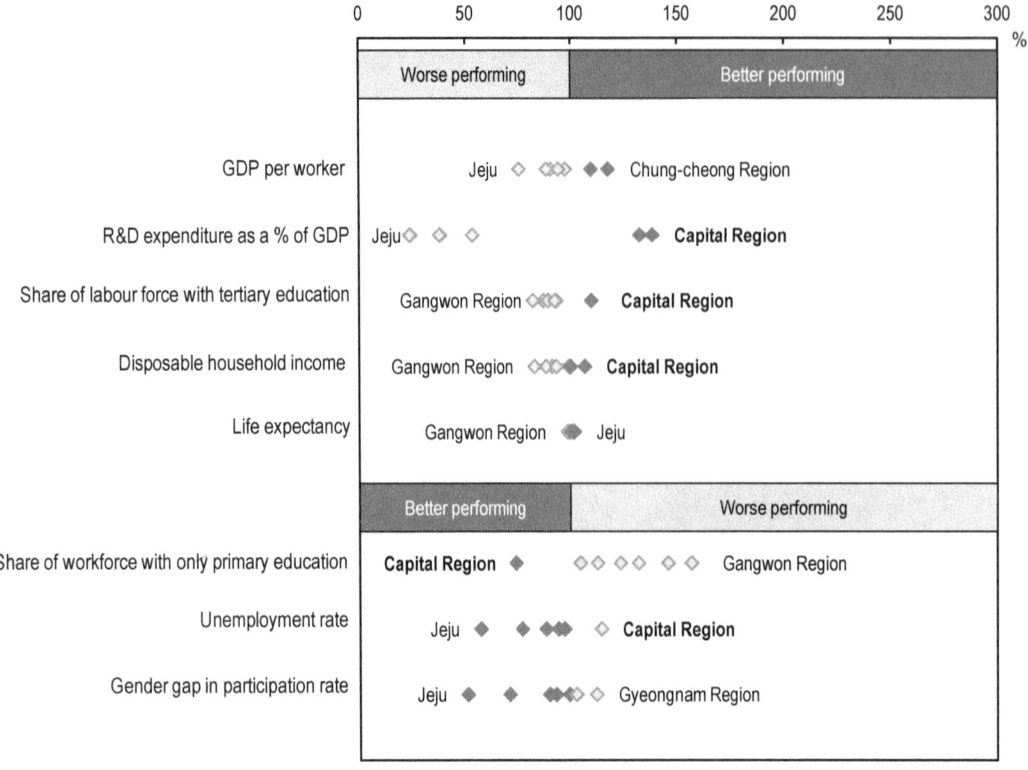

ote: Each diamond represents a TL2 region. All data are for 2014, except GDP per capita, R&D expenditure d disposable household income which are for 2013. Disparity is measured as the difference between the top d bottom region in the country.

urce: OECD (2016e) *OECD Regions at a Glance 2016*, http://dx.doi.org/10.1787/reg_glance-2016-en.

2.2. Seoul is one of the most densely populated cities in the world

eoul is by far the largest city in Korea and the largest metropolitan area in the OECD. ignificant population growth resulted from the rural-urban migration that began in the 950s after the Korean War. Since then, Korea's urban population has increased almost urfold, while the built-up area of the Seoul metropolitan area doubled over the past four ecades (Figure 1.3). In 2014, the Seoul metropolitan area accounted for 5% of the ountry's territory and 50% of the national population. It is the most densely populated nong all OECD metropolitan areas (16 000 inhabitants per km^2), well beyond Tokyo, aris, New York and Mexico City (Figure 1.4).

Figure 1.3. Seoul metropolitan area's built-up area has doubled over the past four decades

Evolution of the built-up area in Seoul metropolitan area, 1975-2014.

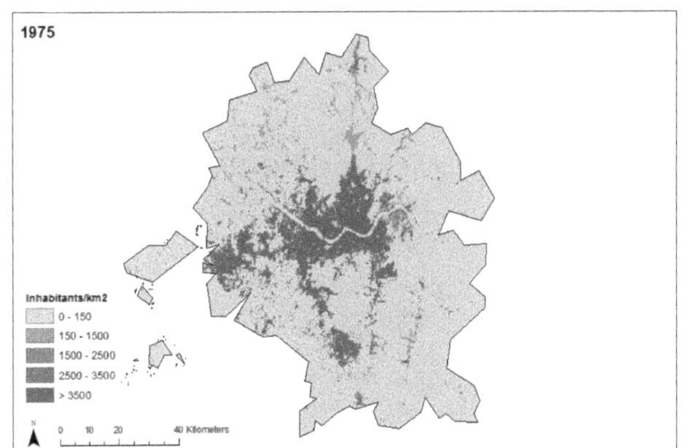

Note: The map represents Seoul's Functional Urban Area
Source: OECD analysis based on the Global Human Settlement (GHS) dataset: http://ghsl.jrc.ec.europa.eu/index.php.

Figure 1.4. Seoul metropolitan area is the most densely populated among OECD metropolitan areas

Population density (inhabitants per km2), 2014

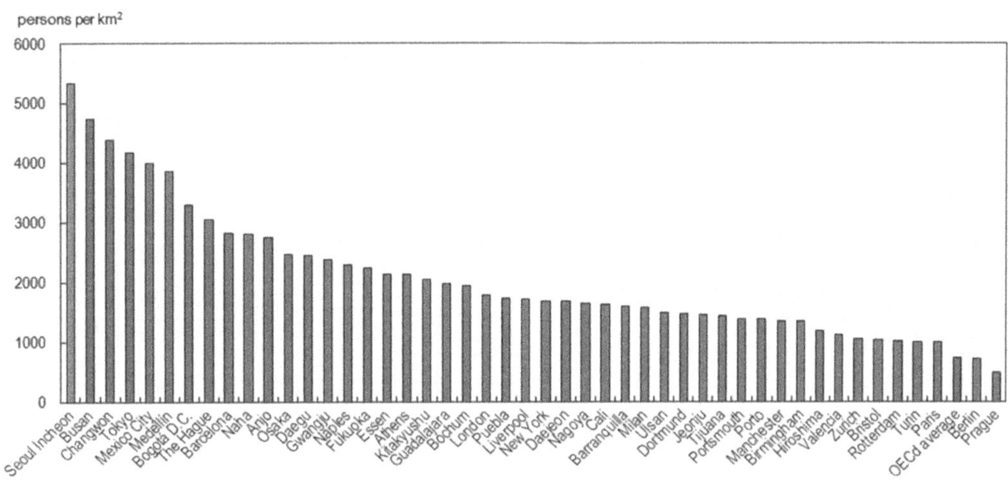

Source: Source: OECD (2017), Metropolitan areas (database) http://dx.doi.org/10.1787/data-00531-en.

1.2.3. A rapidly ageing population, with the elderly more likely to be poor

A rapidly ageing population, which is primarily due to a sharp decline in the fertility rate, poses major demographic challenges for policy makers. Although ageing is common in many OECD countries, Korea has the fastest ageing population in the OECD (OECD, 2016b). The elderly dependency ratio (measured as the population aged 65 and over as a proportion of working age population, 15-64 years old) is expected to increase from 17% in 2014 to over 70% in 2050, well above the OECD average (from 24% in 2014 to 43% in 2050). Moreover, almost half of the Korean elderly population lives below the poverty line, well above the OECD average of 13% (Figure 1.5) (OECD 2016b).

The Seoul metropolitan area concentrates more than one-third of the country's elderly population; this share is larger than the average in OECD metropolitan areas (4%) and Tokyo (25%) and significantly larger than the share of elderly in other Korean metro areas, such as Busan (7%). Elderly residents in Seoul are concentrated in districts with the highest share of low-income households, especially in the centre and northwest part of the city (Figure 1.6).

Figure 1.5. Korea has by far the largest share of elderly poor in the OECD

Share of persons living with less than 50% of median disposable income across OECD countries, by age group (2014)

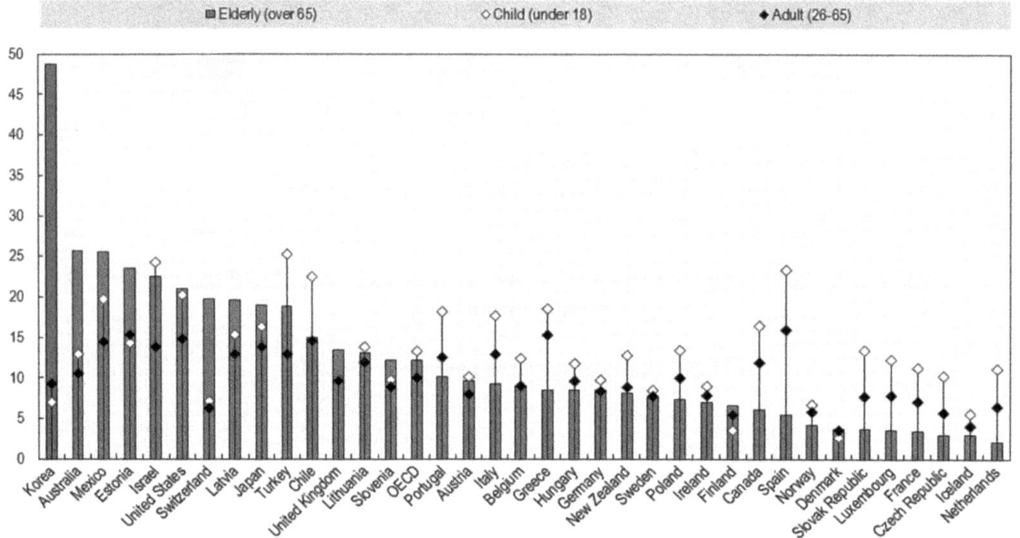

Source: OECD (2016b).

Figure 1.6. Seoul's elderly population resides in predominantly low-income areas

Share of elderly population and low-income households per district in Seoul city.

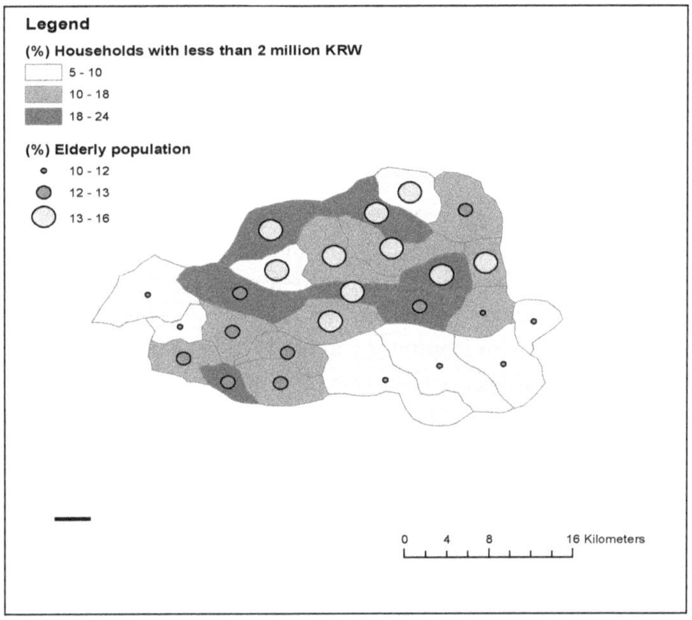

Source: OECD elaboration based on Seoul Metropolitan Government database (2016).

A high level of household debt constrains private consumption and well-being across society, affecting especially the Korean elderly population, self-employed and low-income workers. By 2014, Korea's household debt was 163% of household disposable income, above the OECD average of 137% (OECD, 2016b). According to Kim J. (2015), Korea is the only country in which senior households' total debt-to-income ratio is higher than the population as a whole, unlike major EU countries and the US. By 2014, household debt for the elderly amounted to 73% of their financial assets; the ratio for the over-60 age group in the US and Spain was around 20%.

1.2.4. The lowest fertility rate in the OECD

In parallel to the challenge of ageing, Seoul has the lowest fertility rate in Korea (1 child per women), in a country that records the lowest fertility rate in the OECD (1.2 children per women. The fertility rate in Korea is down from 4.5 in 1970, and compared to a current OECD average (1.7 children per women), below the rate necessary to keep the population constant (2.1) (OECD, 2016b). Some districts within Seoul, such as Jongno or Gwanak, register an even lower fertility rate (0.8).

1.3. Outcomes across four dimensions of Inclusive Growth in Seoul

Korea records important income disparities relative to OECD countries. Korea has the seventh-highest level of income disparity among OECD countries, based on the ratio of the poorest 90th income percentile to the richest 10th (Figure 1.7) (OECD, 2016a). High income inequality reflects large gaps in productivity and wages between large conglomerates and small firms (Chapter 3), manufacturing and services, and regular and non-regular workers[2] (OECD, 2016a). In particular, the dualistic structure of the labour market has resulted in high wage inequality and a high relative poverty rate (14% in 2014, the eighth-highest in the OECD). Given the problems in small firms and services, Korea's overall labour productivity is only 55% of the top half of OECD countries (OECD, 2016a).

Although robust data on income inequality are not available at the level of Seoul, there is clear evidence that some groups face important disparities in terms of income and wages, as well as in a number of non-income dimensions. This section delves deeper into the challenges facing specific groups – namely the elderly, women, youth and migrant workers. Building on ongoing OECD work on inequalities in cities (Box 1.1) and regional well-being (Box 1.2), the analysis goes beyond income to assess outcomes in Seoul along the four dimensions of the *New York Proposal for Inclusive Growth in Cities* and the *Paris Action Plan for Inclusive Growth in Cities*: 1) education, 2) labour market, 3) housing and the urban environment, and 4) infrastructure and public services. Although the policy competencies of local governments vary across countries, these are four policy areas in which cities – often in partnership other levels of government – may have some capacity to intervene to address inequalities.

Figure 1.7. Regional disparities are relatively high in Korea, and have been on the rise

Gini index of inequality of GDP per capita across TL3 regions, 2000 and 2013.

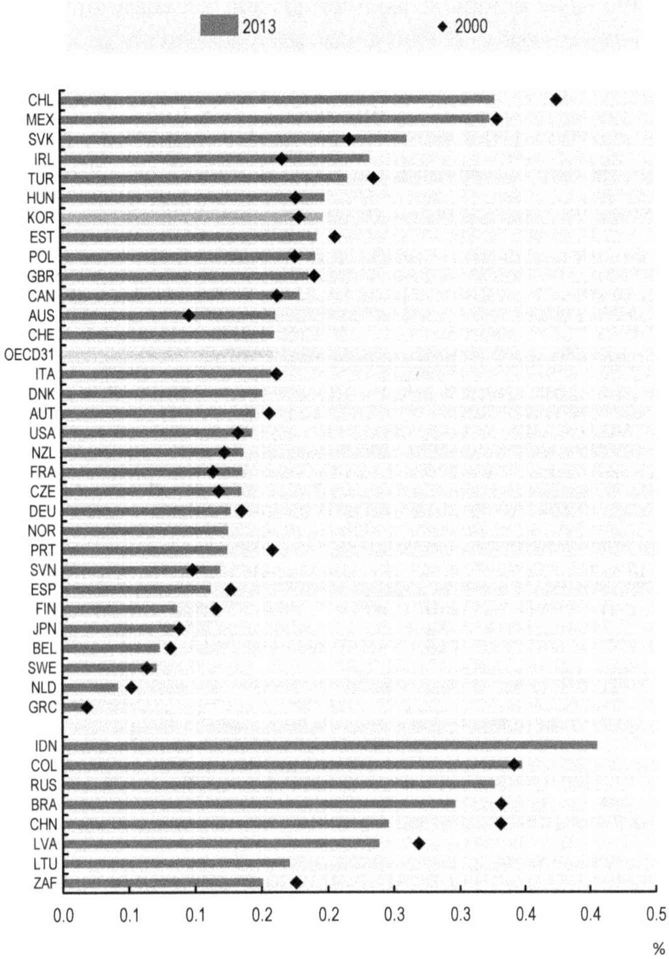

Note: Regions within the 34 OECD countries are classified on two territorial levels reflecting the administrative organisation of countries. The 391 OECD large (TL2) regions represent the first administrative tier of subnational government. The 2 197 OECD small (TL3) regions are contained in a TL2 region. TL3 regions correspond to administrative regions, with the exception of Australia, Canada, Germany and the United States. Data for period 2000-13. TL3 regions. Australia, Canada, Chile, Mexico, Turkey and the United States TL2 regions. Germany Non Official Grids regions. Brazil, China, Colombia, Indonesia, Russian Federation and South Africa TL2 regions. Regional GVA for Turkey. Regional GDP is not available for Iceland and Israel. For China, data for the Special Administrative Region of Hong Kong, the Special Administrative Region of Macau and Chinese Taipei are excluded. First available years: Japan and India 2001; Mexico 2003; China 2004. Last available year: Austria, Brazil, China, Colombia, Estonia, Finland, France, Germany, Hungary, Indonesia, Ireland, Italy, Japan, Latvia, Lithuania, Norway, Poland, Russian Federation, Spain, Sweden and Switzerland 2012. Information on data for Israel: http://dx.doi.org/10.1787/888932315602.

Source: OECD (2016e), *OECD Regions at a Glance 2016*, OECD Publishing, Paris. http://dx.doi.org/10.1787/reg_glance-2016-en.

Box 1.2. A framework for measuring regional well-being

Measuring well-being is a complex task, comprising a variety of dimensions, including having a good job, enjoying social relations with other people, living in a safe neighbourhood, and so on. Some of these dimensions of well-being are linked to the characteristics of individual citizens, while others have more to do with the region they live in. The combination of the two affects overall well-being. Policies that take into account regional differences, beyond national averages, can therefore have a greater impact on improving the well-being of the country as a whole.

The OECD has developed a framework and a database to measure well-being at the subnational level, in all 395 regions of the OECD, where regions generally correspond to the first tier of subnational government. The database covers 11 well-being dimensions and includes also self-reported experience of well-being, such as sense of community and satisfaction with life. This framework builds on two stands of work: the OECD Better Life Initiative and on the OECD Regional Well-being Database.

The potential use of subnational well-being metrics for policymaking has stimulated several regions and cities to launch initiatives integrating well-being measurement in policy design and monitoring. For example, the Region of Southern Denmark promoted an initiative called *The Good Life* to measure well-being in all municipalities and help policy makers identify areas for policy prioritisation, raise social awareness and improve policy coherence across different policy domains (OECD, 2014).

Source: OECD (2014b) *How is Life in Your Region? Measuring Regional and Local Well-being for Policy Making*, OECD Publishing, Paris, http://dx.doi.org/10.1787/9789264217416-en.

1.3.1. Education

An inclusive education system is one that aims to expand opportunities for people of all ages and backgrounds to develop their human capital, acquire relevant skills and improve their employment and overall life prospects (OECD, 2016c and 2016d). While Korea has strong overall education outcomes and positive equity indicators in education, there is some evidence of spatial sorting by education levels across neighbourhoods. Moreover, disparities in education become more evident in later years of schooling, notably due to the prevalence of supplementary education that is considered essential to gain access to prestigious universities and high-paying employment. These institutions tend to be privately operated and located in higher-income neighbourhoods.

A strong inclusive education framework at national level

A strong policy framework at national level has helped to ensure excellent education outcomes and equitable access to education in the early years. Korea is among the OECD's top-performing countries in the Programme for International Student Assessment (PISA) and has positive equity indicators for 15 year-olds (OECD, 2016f). This means that socio-economic background has a weaker impact on student performance in Korea, compared to the OECD average in PISA 2012, and this has been the case since PISA 2003. The Korean government has put in place a number of policies to promote equity in education, most notable in the early years. Coverage of early childhood education and care is very high (OECD, 2016f). The cost of pre-school education for all 3-5 years-olds is supported by the national government, regardless of household income.

Nonetheless, in Seoul there is evidence of spatial sorting by education level across the city. In Seoul, districts with the highest income levels correspond to those with a large share of households with a bachelor degree and above (Figure 1.8). For instance, the district of Gangnam-gu records the largest share of households with at least a bachelor degree and the smallest share of poorer households. In addition, resources for education differ depending on the district in which the public school is located. Schools in richer areas have larger budgets. For example, in 2010, the Gangnam district in southern Seoul had a USD 25 million budget, whereas the district of Eunpyung, a relatively poorer area, had only USD 3 million (Shin, 2013).

Figure 1.8. Residents living in rich areas have a higher level of education

Share of low income households and higher education level by district in Seoul

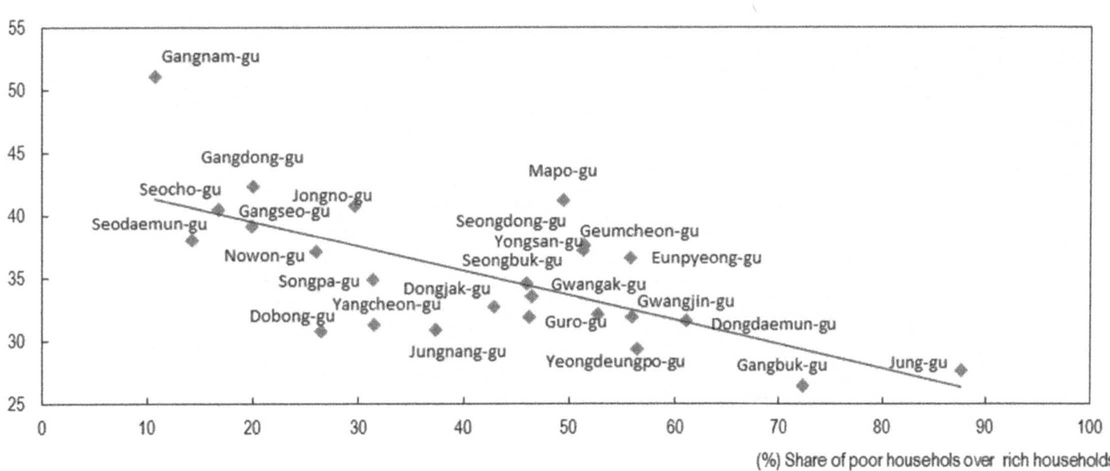

Note: Poor households are defined as the households earning in average less than KRW 2 million per month (approx. USD 1 800) while rich households are defined as those earning more than KRW 5 million (USD 4 500).

Source: Seoul Metropolitan Government (2016), 2015 Seoul Survey, The Seoul Institute.

Challenges for lower-income students to compete given the importance of private supplementary schooling

Disparities in education become more evident in later years of schooling, notably due to the prevalence of supplementary education that is considered essential to gain access to prestigious universities and high-paying employment. Korea has the highest percentage of students attending after-school lessons in mathematics (76%) in the OECD, compared to an OECD average of 34% (OECD, 2014c). Despite numerous government interventions, an exceptionally high level of private spending on supplementary education (after school lessons) and preparation for the third-level admission process remains a prominent feature of the education system, particularly in the Capital Region. The entrance exam into the three most prestigious "SKY" universities (Seoul National, Korea and Yonsei) is perceived as a significant sign of social status for most Korean families and affects an individual's prospects for securing a high paying job in one of the *chaebols* (family-owned business conglomerates; Chapter 3).

In Seoul, supplementary education institutions are located in higher-income neighbourhoods, and the top students are found to have spent more resources in supplemental education than their lowest-performing peers. Figure 1.9 shows that the number of institutes of supplementary education which are preponderantly private, are mostly located in high-income neighbourhoods. In fact, OECD (2014c) found that students in the top 10% of their class spend double the financial resources in supplementary education than students in the bottom 20%. The share of private expenditure on education in Korea (the share of household's total expenditure allocated to education) is among the highest in OECD, particularly at the tertiary level: 73% of spending on tertiary education came from private sources in 2011, compared with an OECD average of 31%. By contrast, annual public expenditure per student on tertiary educational institutions (USD 3 076) in Korea was much lower than the OECD average of USD 9 221 (OECD, 2014d).

Figure 1.9. Supplementary education institutions are located in higher-income neighbourhoods

Share of households with higher education and number of institutes of supplementary education by district in Seoul

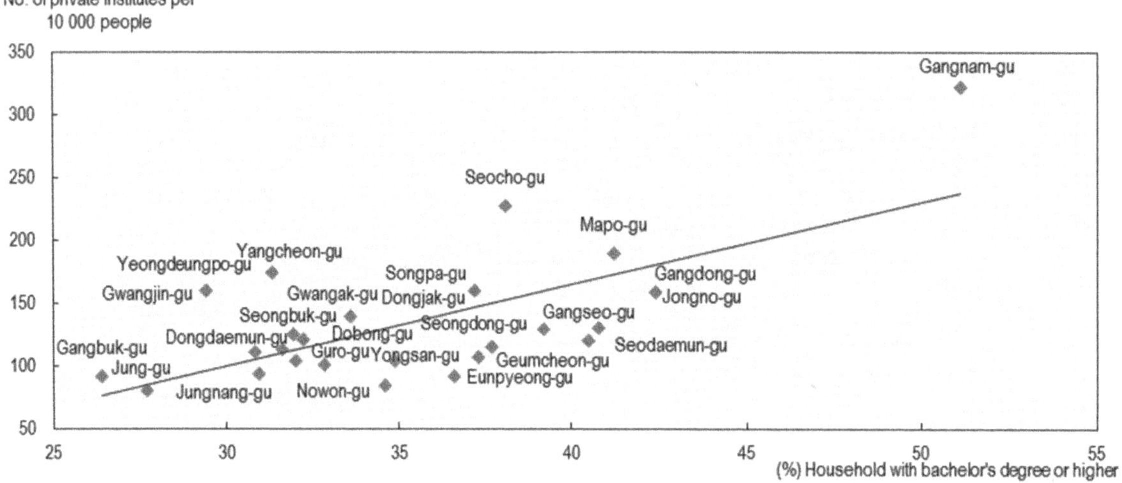

Source: Seoul Metropolitan Government (2016), 2015 Seoul Survey, The Seoul Institute.

Given the importance of the private education market in Korea, the Seoul Metropolitan Government (SMG) has implemented several initiatives to bridge educational gaps. For example, the government provides financial support to pay for textbooks, school supplies, admission fees, tuition and – for high school students – lunch for students from households with an income level below 50% of the median. Other programmes focused on supporting students from low-income families are geared toward early childhood development and student mentorship by university students.

1.3.2. Labour market

An inclusive labour market affords people of all social and ethnic backgrounds access to quality employment opportunities and provides all individuals the chance to contribute to the economy and to share in the benefits of economic growth. While Korea has excellent levels of education and skills, labour productivity is the fourth lowest among OECD countries and the employment rates of youth and women rank among the lowest in the OECD (OECD, 2016b).

A dualistic labour market, divided between regular and non-regular workers

Korea's labour market is divided into regular and non-regular workers. For more than a decade, non-regular employees (such as fixed-term, part-time, and dispatched workers) have accounted for one-third of the total employees in the country (OECD, 2016a). Non-regular workers earn around 64% of the hourly wage of regular workers, even though their skill levels are similar. The wage gap of individuals brings inequality at the household level as well. Households headed by a non-regular worker suffer from strained family budgets and higher levels of household debt. The relative poverty rate is more than 10% higher in non-regular households (OECD, 2016a). Further, non-regular workers often have weaker social protections. While most regular workers in Korea receive the major social insurance schemes including health insurance, only around a half of non-regular workers are covered.

The disparities in wages and working conditions between regular and non-regular workers are observed in Seoul as well. In 2016, non-regular employees accounted for 32.1% of the total working population in the city. The monthly wage of non-regular workers in Seoul amounted to KRW 1.3 million (USD 1 300) less than that of regular employees, and only 41% of non-regular workers are covered by health insurance (Seoul Metropolitan Government, 2017).

A large share of young people are unemployed, regardless of educational attainment

Youth unemployment is high in Korea. Around 18% of young people in Korea (15-29 years old) were neither employed nor in education or training (NEET) in 2015, compared to the OECD average of 15% (OECD, 2016f). Although the youth unemployment rate in Seoul city (10.3%) is lower than in many of its international peers such as London (17.9%) (EY, 2016) or New York (10.5%), it is nevertheless 2.4 times higher than the unemployment rate in the Seoul metro area (4.3%). Moreover, approximately 17% of the youth labour force has experienced prolonged (one-to-three years) unemployment.

Labour market inactivity rates among Korean youth are among the highest in the OECD. This trend holds true even among well-educated youth: one-fifth of Koreans aged 25-34 with tertiary education were not active in the labour force in 2015 (OECD, 2016f). As Figure 1.10 shows, youth in Seoul between 15-29 years of age are more likely to be unemployed than the rest of population, regardless of the level of education. Indeed, OECD (2016f) found that unemployment rates are lower for older Koreans than younger Koreans at all levels of educational attainment. For example, 2.4% of 55-64 year-olds with below secondary education were unemployed, compared to 10% of 25-34 year-olds. Many young people work in part-time jobs (Seoul Metropolitan Government, 2017).

Figure 1.10. Youth unemployment in Seoul is higher than the total unemployment rate

Rate of youth unemployment and total unemployment in Seoul, 2014-16

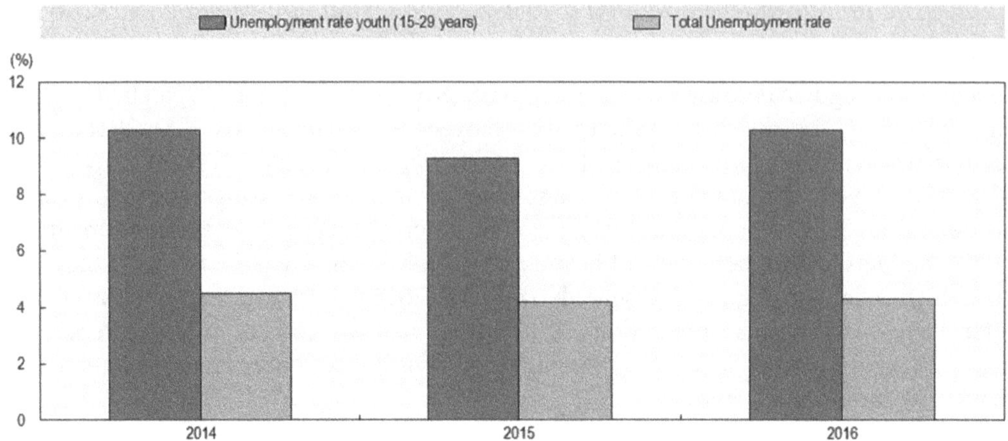

Source: Seoul Metropolitan Government (2016).

A large gender gap in the labour market prevents equal opportunities for women

The considerable educational progress that Korea has achieved in recent decades has not fully translated into better labour market outcomes for women. In part, this reflects the inheritance of Korea's economic model of working very long hours, which makes it difficult to combine employment with family responsibilities and can be a barrier to sustained career progress for women. Korea registers the widest wage gap between men and women among OECD countries. Korean women are paid 63% of men's average wage, far lower than the average wage gap of OECD countries (85%). Given the seniority wage system and labour market dualism (regular versus non-regular employment), the loss in wages and career prospects for those who temporarily leave the labour force results in a very large "motherhood penalty" (OECD, 2013). The large gap in Korea is surprising, given that the university graduation rate for women is higher than that for men among those aged 25 to 34 – the highest, in fact, in the OECD (OECD, 2016b).

As Figure 1.11 shows, Seoul city also records a large gender gap in labour force participation, compared to other large cities from OECD and EU countries. Female labour participation rates in Korea have remained about the same today relative to 20 years ago (55% compared with an OECD average of 65%), with only 10% of all managerial positions being held by women compared with one-third across the OECD (OECD, 2013). The gender disparity in the labour force is considerable: of the working age population in Seoul city, 53% of women participate in economic activities compared to 73% of men.

Figure 1.11. Seoul has one of the highest gender gaps in labour force participation among selected world cities

Percentage-point gap in the labour force participation (male-female), 2014

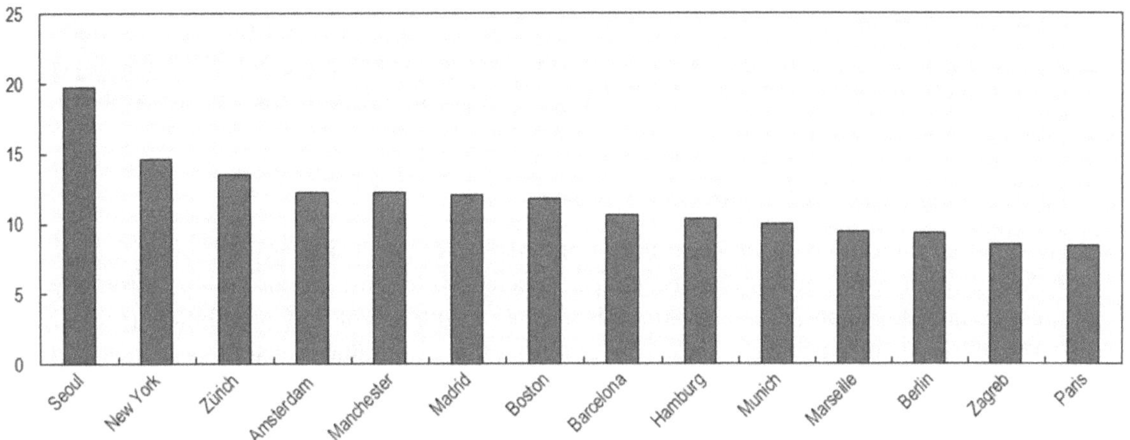

Note: Data for Marseille and Paris are for 2013. Data for Manchester are 2015. Data for all other cities are for 2014.

Source: Eurostat (2017), *Cities and Functional Urban Areas* (database); BLS (2015), *Women in the labour force: a databook* (database).

The elderly are often self-employed or in low-quality jobs, contributing to a high poverty rate for seniors

Workers are forced out of firms at around age 53 on average in Korea, leaving the elderly populations to transition into self-employment, low-quality and/or low-paid jobs (OECD, 2016a). Early retirement and low-quality jobs are a factor in leading older populations into poverty. The relative poverty rate of people over 50 in Korea is 15.5%, around 1.5 times higher than the OECD average; this figure jumps to 49.6% for the population over age 65 (OECD, 2016a). Furthermore, one third of Korean seniors are characterised as living in absolute poverty, which could be related to a high elderly suicide rate in the country (OECD, 2016a).

In Seoul, the number of workers aged over 65 has increased from 207 000 people in 2009 to 306 000 people in 2014, which accounts for 27% of the total senior population. However, as the national trend shows, they are mostly self-employed or employed in low-quality jobs (Yoon, 2016). In addition, even though both the relative and absolute poverty rate of persons over age 65 is lower in Seoul compared to the national average, inequality levels among the elderly population – between very wealthy seniors and very poor seniors – is higher in Seoul than in other Korean cities. The senior poverty rate is especially high among women, the less-educated, and those living alone (Kim K.H., 2015).

Foreign workers face significant challenges in the labour market

Foreigners account for less than 2% of the total population, among the five lowest in the OECD and well below the OECD average (13%) (OECD, 2017c). While Seoul city hosts 65% of the foreign population in Korea, migrants represent only a small share of Seoul city's total population (3%). Seoul's share is considerably smaller than that of New York

City (38%) (NYC Department of City Planning, 2015), and just below that of Tokyo (3.3%) (Tokyo Metropolitan Government, 2016). More than 70% of Seoul's foreign population are originally from China (Seoul Metropolitan Government, 2016).

Foreign workers recorded an unemployment rate of 40% in 2016 in Seoul city, equivalent to ten times the overall unemployment rate of 4%. More than half of foreign workers earn less than KRW 2 million per month (approximately USD 1 750), well below the average wage of non-migrant residents in Seoul (KRW 3.2 million) (OECD, 2015; Seoul Metropolitan Government, 2017). In Seoul, the foreign workforce tends to be employed in unskilled jobs in the service sector (such as restaurants) and the construction and manufacturing industries.

1.3.3. Housing and the urban environment

The spatial dimension is another important aspect of inclusive growth in cities: an inclusive urban environment can be characterised by access to good-quality, affordable housing in safe, healthy neighbourhoods for all segments of the population (OECD, 2016c; 2016d). In particular, access to good-quality affordable housing is a means to prevent poverty and social exclusion, encourage equal opportunities through better access to health, education and social capital, and promote inclusion in the labour market.

Despite progress, low-income group, seniors and migrants are more likely to live in low-quality housing

Although the housing cost burden for households in Korea is low, estimated at 10% of disposable income compared to the OECD average of 17%[3], the provision of quality affordable housing remains a challenge in Korea, especially for the younger population. Moreover, within Korea, the housing price-income ratio is much higher in the Seoul metropolitan area relative to other metropolitan areas in the country and the national average (Figure 1.12). Difficulties to access quality affordable housing has led many young people to delay marriage and starting a family (MOLIT, 2017).

Figure 1.12. Housing in the Seoul metropolitan area is much less affordable than elsewhere in Korea

Housing price-income ratio by region in Korea, 2006-2016

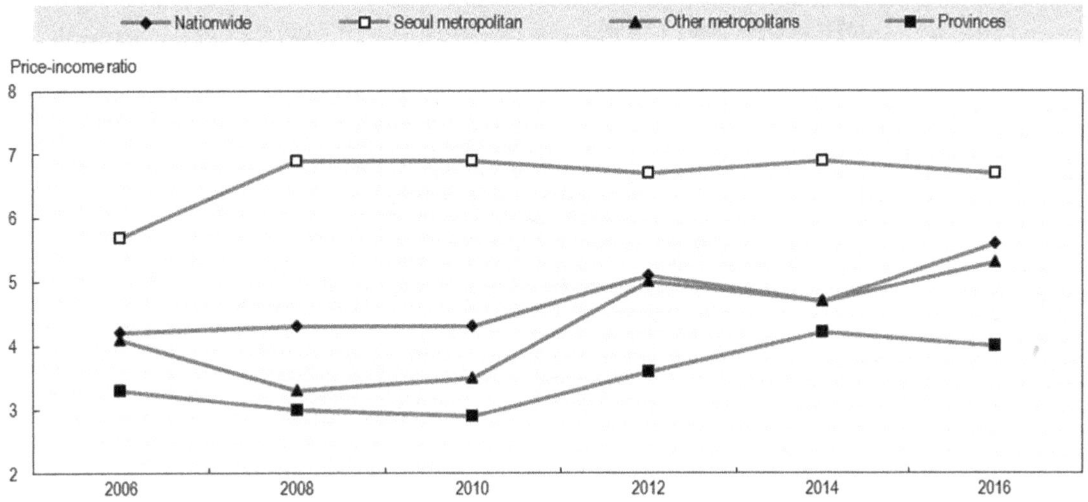

Note: Data for Seoul refer to the metropolitan area. Income data refer to median income.
Source: Ministry of Land, Infrastructure and Transport (MOLIT) (2016), 2016 Korea Housing Survey.

In Seoul, people living in low-income districts tend to live in dwellings of no more than $20m^2$. Moreover, many illegal settlements were constructed without permits before the 1990s. In an effort to combat people living in illegal dwellings, the city responded by building "citizens' apartments" to house illegal settlement residents. However, despite efforts, there are still many illegal settlements located in the central part of the city, which are also characterised by low levels of income (Figure 1.13).

Figure 1.13. Low-income level districts have a larger share of illegal settlements in Seoul

Concentration of illegal settlements by district in Seoul, 2015

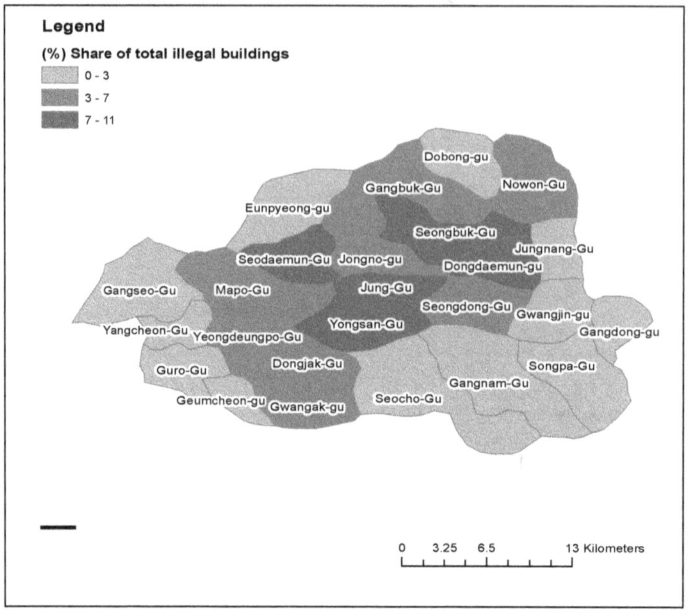

Source: Seoul Metropolitan Government database (2016).

Housing a rapidly ageing population is another major policy concern. Although Korea has made significant progress toward improving the quality of housing for seniors, nearly one quarter of seniors live in homes that fail to meet the Korean government's minimum standards relating to floor space, the environment and housing facilities (OECD, 2012b). Much work remains to be done to improve housing quality for Korean seniors. This existing challenge will be exacerbated in the coming decades with the increasing dependency of seniors relative to the working-age population.

Migrants and foreign workers also face housing challenges. They tend to live in non-residential buildings, including factories and shopping centres, where two or three people may share a single room and bathroom (OECD, 2012b). Furthermore, nearly 10% of foreign households with over three people live in single rooms, extremely high compared to the Korean average (0.27%). More than half of foreign workers earn less than KRW 2 million per month (approximately USD 1 750), below the KRW 3.2 million average wage of non-migrant residents in Seoul (OECD, 2015; Seoul Metropolitan Government, 2017).

Air pollution affects mostly low-income neighbourhoods and the elderly

Environmental challenges pose particular risks for the health and well-being of low-income and elderly populations. While policy interventions by the Seoul Metropolitan Government have helped to reduce air pollution levels in the metropolitan area over the past decade, air quality remains a pressing environmental challenge, and one that tends to disproportionately affect already vulnerable groups. At national level, Korea has some of the highest rates of air pollution among the OECD countries. Exposure to fine particulate matter ($PM_{2.5}$) and ground level ozone are particularly severe. It is estimated that the number of premature deaths caused by air pollution in Korea rose by 29% between 2005 and 2013, and the number is projected to almost triple by 2060 (OECD, 2017d).

In Seoul Metropolitan Area, PM_{10} and NO_2 levels decreased by half between 2001 and 2014 as a result of pollution mitigation policies adopted in 2005 and to the air pollutant emission cap management system introduced in 2008 (OECD, 2017d). However, the Seoul Metropolitan Area recorded the third-highest average levels of fine particulate matter, $PM_{2.5}$ (27ug/m^{3-}) among 291 OECD metro areas between 2012 and 2014 (Figure 1.14), with levels well beyond World Health Organization (WHO) standards (10 ug/m^3 annual average) (see Chapter 2).

Figure 1.14. Air pollution in Seoul Metropolitan Area is among the poorest in OECD metro areas

Air pollution levels in selected OECD metro areas, three-year average 2012-2014, PM 2.5 (µg/m³)

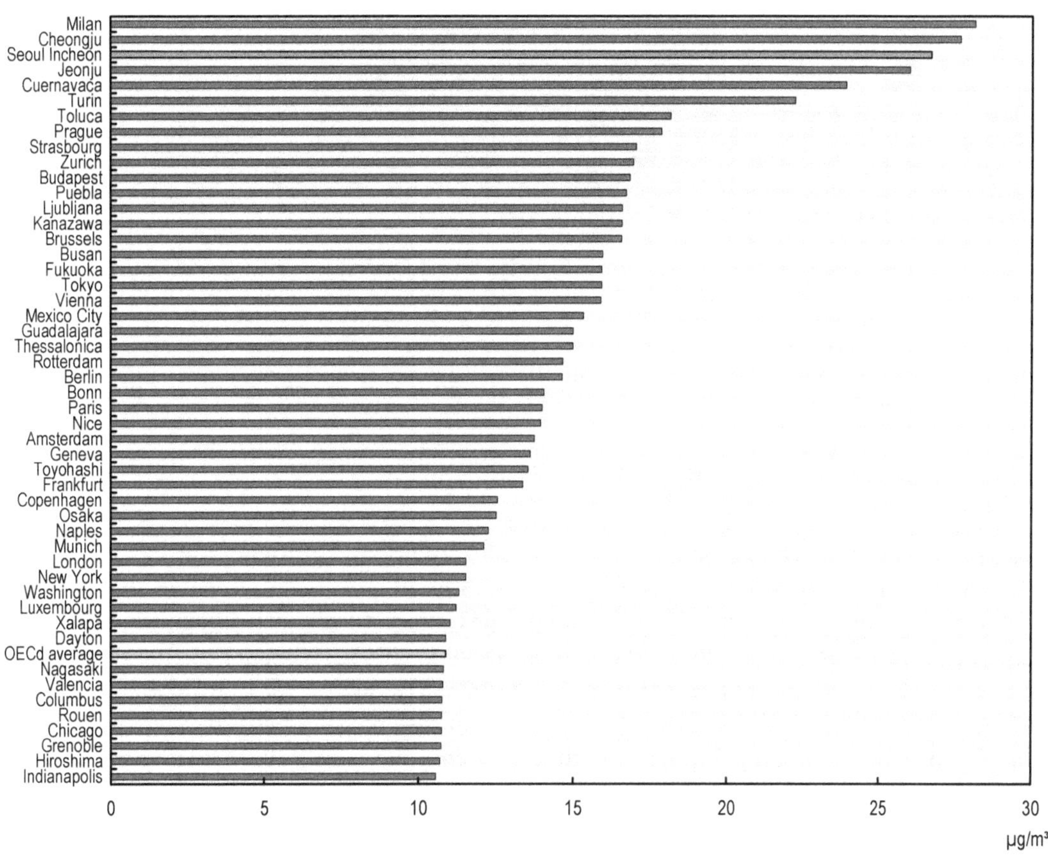

Source: OECD (2015), "Metropolitan areas", OECD Regional Statistics (database), http://dx.doi.org/10.1787/data-00531-en.

In Seoul, high levels of air pollution have led to lower quality of life, particularly in poorer neighbourhoods. Figure 1.15 shows that districts with a higher share of low-income families also experience higher levels of pollution. In addition, these lower-income districts are also those characterised by a larger share of senior citizens, who have a higher risk of having health challenges, including death, resulting from air pollution, especially on hot days (Kim et al., 2015; Son et al., 2012).

Figure 1.15. Low-income districts tend to be more affected by air pollution in Seoul

Share of low-income households and air pollution level by district in Seoul, 2015

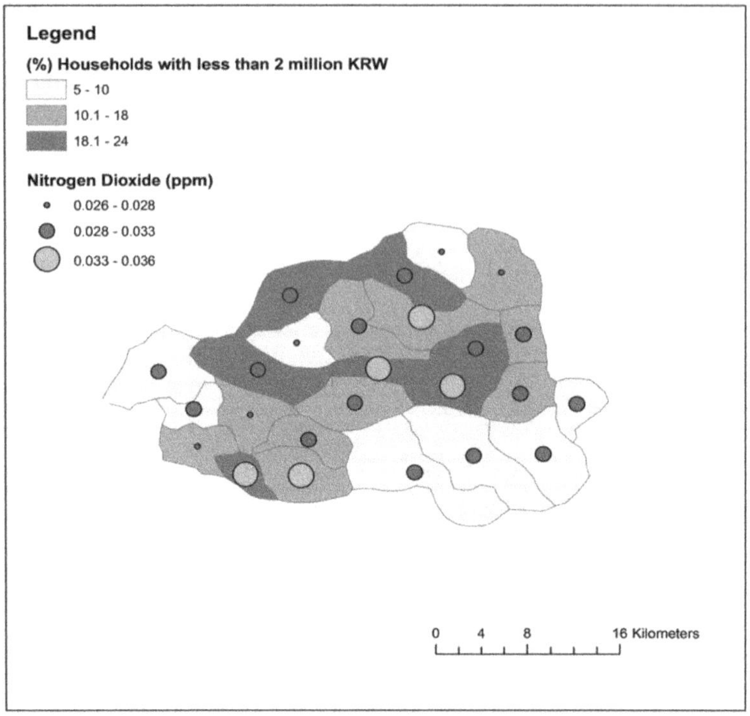

Note: KRW refers to South Korean Won. KRW 2 million per month is approximatively USD 1 800.
Source: Seoul Metropolitan Government (2016).

Traffic congestion is one major cause of air pollution, as Seoul has a far higher percentage of pollutant emissions from automobiles than other regions in the country (World Health Organization, 2011). Automobiles generate seven times more CO_2 than buses and 15 times more than the subway in Seoul in 2013. Exposure to fine particulate matter ($PM_{2.5}$) and ground level ozone is particularly severe. It is estimated that the number of premature deaths caused by air pollution rose by 29% between 2005 and 2013, and the number is projected to almost triple by 2060, due partly to an ageing population and urbanisation (OECD, 2017d).

Adaptation challenges: Seoul records low green space per capita

Seoul is one of ten metropolitan areas in the OECD with the lowest green space per capita. As Figure 1.16 shows, when compared by the level of density, Seoul ranks last in terms of green area provision. However, this is not an exclusive problem for certain areas of the metro area, as all districts in Seoul face the same problem.

Figure 1.16. Seoul Metropolitan Area lacks green space

Green area per person and density in OECD metropolitan areas

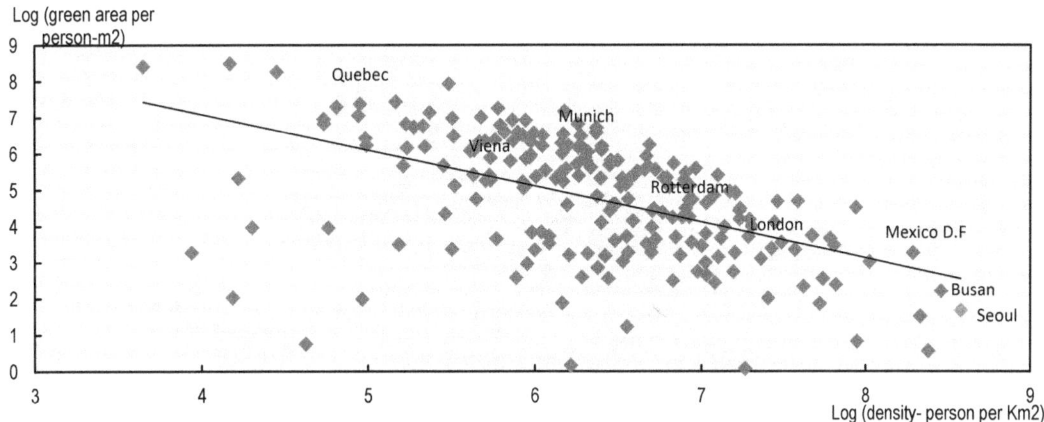

Note: Data do not include the United States due to low density.
Source: OECD (2017), Metropolitan areas (database) http://dx.doi.org/10.1787/data-00531-en.

1.3.4. Access to public services

Access to quality infrastructure and public services is another key pillar of inclusive growth in cities. Access to public transport is, overall, extremely high in Seoul. Access to quality drinking water is a challenge for lower-income households, while access to public health care is equitable across neighbourhoods in Seoul, yet many elderly and low-income populations face financial constraints.

Seoul's public transport system is highly effective overall, with some gaps for women and the elderly

With few exceptions, Seoul has one of the top urban public transport systems in the world, providing the vast majority of urban dwellers with excellent access to jobs and services. Over 80% of the city's population lives within 10 minutes of a bus stop and almost 20% within 10 minutes of a train station (OECD, 2017e). Among TL2 regions in Korea, Seoul registers the highest level of accessibility to public transport (Figure 1.17) (OECD, 2017e). Some gaps remain: accessibility to bus stops in Seoul tends to be higher in areas with higher average incomes; and the elderly in Seoul tend to live in areas further away from a bus stop, which is contrary to trends in most other Korean regions (OECD, 2017e). Nevertheless, Seoul's public transport system provides strong coverage overall, and evidence suggests that improvements in public transport management over the past few years have helped reduce spatial segregation and boosted access to jobs and public services (OECD, 2017e).

Figure 1.17. Seoul registers a high level of accessibility to public transport

Public transport accessibility in Seoul in 2010

Source: OECD (2017), *Urban Transport Governance and Inclusive Development in Korea*, OECD Publishing, Paris, http://dx.doi.org/10.1787/9789264272637-en .

The Seoul Metropolitan Government has implemented programmes to improve the accessibility of some vulnerable groups to public transport. The programmes target the disabled and visually impaired, pregnant women, low-income students, and the elderly. Some of the measures include the installation of Braille blocks and elevators in underground stations, improved guidance systems increased visibility of priority seats, and the introduction of buses adapted for populations with reduced mobility. Efforts to boost financial accessibility have also been introduced, notably reduced fares for older students who return to their studies later in life.

Disparities in access to high quality tap water remain

Seoul is an international leader in monitoring water quality, overseeing more than 163 substances in water, which meets the international WHO recommendations and far surpasses the average monitoring level in Korea (83 substances monitored). Since 2011, Seoul Metropolitan Government has strengthened the assessment of tap water quality in households with the aim of replacing outdated water pipes and improving the general environmental conditions of the water supply. Nonetheless, poorer households are more likely to face challenges with respect to water quality in Seoul (Figure 1.18). Districts with a higher proportion of poor households registered a lower score in the 2016 inspection programme.

Figure 1.18. Low-income districts have lower quality tap water score in Seoul

Share of low-income households and water quality by district in Seoul, 2016

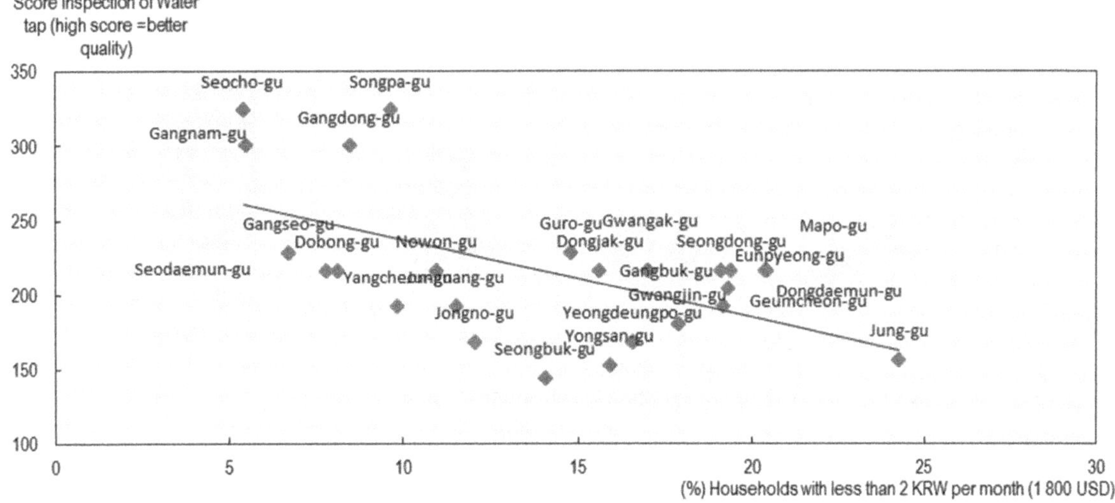

Note: Score is taken form the inspection result 2016 that analyses 5 aspects: Turbidity, pH, Residual chlorine, coliform group and Escherichia coli level.
Source: Seoul Metropolitan Government, Electricity, Gas and Water supply database (2016).

The elderly and less educated residents face financial hurdles to access healthcare

The provision of public health institutions is equitably distributed across Seoul, with one centre per district, and even more public health centres located in low-income districts. Private health centres are concentrated in the higher-income central and southeast parts of the city. While Koreans benefit from universal health care insurance and physical access to health care may not be a problem, some medical needs remain unmet due to the high level of out-of-pocket payments required (e.g. for direct payment for hospitalisations, outpatient visits, dental treatment, surgery, prescription drugs, nursing care). This constitutes a financial burden, especially for the elderly and residents with lower income levels (Figure 1.19, Figure 1.20). This is all the more challenging in the context of rapid population ageing.

Figure 1.19. The elderly face financial difficulties in meeting their medical needs

(%) proportion of people who did not have access to hospital due to financial constraints, average 2011-2014.

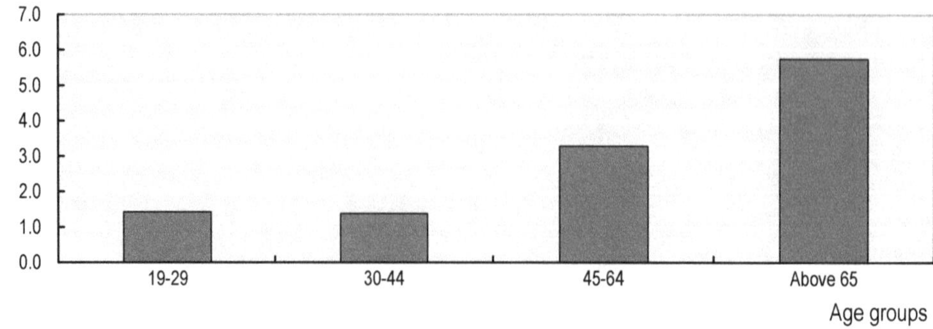

Source: Seoul Metropolitan Government and the Seoul Institute (2016).

Figure 1.20. Less educated Seoul residents face financial barriers to access medical services

(%) proportion of people who did not have access to hospitals due to financial constraints, average 2011-2014.

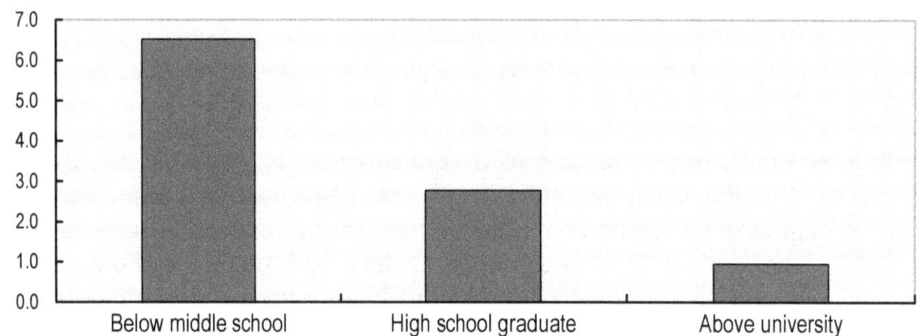

Source: Seoul Metropolitan Government and the Seoul Institute (2016).

Seoul Metropolitan Government aims to increase the level of accessibility of vulnerable groups to welfare services. Thus, it has increased the number of personnel dedicated to work on welfare at the level of *dong* (smallest administrative unit) as part of the "Visiting Community Service Centre" Programme. This initiative aims to deliver more practical welfare benefits to citizens. Between 2015 and 2016, the welfare workforce visited 72% of the population aged over 65 and 88% of the households facing economic crisis. The government has also reinforced support services for self-reliance and social participation of the disabled, introduced the "Seoul Baby Health First Step Programme" to bridge the healthcare gap and ensure equal access to healthcare services for children and mothers.

Energy poverty affects one in ten households

In addition to a heightened vulnerability to climate risks that will be explored in Chapter 2, energy poverty is a challenge for more than 10% of households in Seoul. This means that around one in ten cannot afford heat or air conditioning, a worrisome statistic given the prospect of more extreme weather events in the context of a changing climate (Chapter 2). Low incomes, combined with low energy efficiency dwellings and home appliances, create a burden for poorer households. Moreover, beyond the exposure to climate risks, there is ample evidence to suggest that low-income and other vulnerable populations will face additional hurdles in responding to and recovering from climate damages. In light of the city's rapidly ageing population – and the relative poverty of seniors – the elderly are at serious risk.

1.4. Towards a people-centred policy agenda for Inclusive Growth in Seoul

Seoul inhabitants benefit from high quality public services, including education, health and public transport, yet a number of challenges remain. The city faces a rapid and massive demographic transition, a rigid labour market that poses significant barriers for certain populations and firms and, as will be further explored in the next Chapter, a changing climate that risks exacerbating existing inequalities and disadvantages. Along with policies at the national level to address these critical policy challenges, SMG has made a concerted effort to promote a growth paradigm that is more inclusive, climate-resilient and low-carbon.

Notes

[1] For further explanation of OECD-EU functional urban area methodology, see OECD (2012a).

[2] Non-regular workers earn around 64% of the hourly wage of regular workers even though their skill levels are similar, and often have weaker social protections relative to regular workers.

[3] For further information see: OECD Affordable Housing Database (2017b).

References

ACI; Airports Council International (9 September 2016), "Airports Council International releases 2015 World Airport Traffic Report. The busiest become busier; the year of the international hub airport", *ACI Media Releases*, www.aci.aero/News/Releases/Most-Recent/2016/09/09/Airports-Council-International-releases-2015-World-Airport-Traffic-Report-The-busiest-become-busier-the-year-of-the-international-hub-airport.

BLS; The Bureau of Labor Statitics (2015), *Women in the labour force: a databook* (database), www.bls.gov (accessed August 17, 2017).

EY (2016), *The employment landscape for young people in the UK*, Ernst & Young LLP, London, www.ey.com/Publication/vwLUAssets/Employment_landscape_for_young_people_in_the_UK/$FILE/Employment%20landscape%20for%20young%20people%20in%20the%20UK%20-%20final%20report.pdf.

Eurostat (2017), *Cities and Functional Urban Areas* (database), http://ec.europa.eu/eurostat/web/cities/data/database (accessed August 17, 2017).

Kim, C., Y. Lim, A. Woodward and H. Kim (2015), *Heat-Attributable Deaths between 1992 and 2009 in Seoul, South Korea*, https://dx.doi.org/10.1371%2Fjournal.pone.0118577.

Kim, J. (2015), *Why Household Debt Held by Korean Seniors is Problematic: An International Comparison*, Korea Development Institute, Sejong, www.accessecon.com/Pubs/EB/2016/Volume36/EB-16-V36-I4-P203.pdf.

Kim, K. H. (2015), *Socio-economic deficiency of the elderly in Seoul, and the strategies to develop senior welfare policy*, The Seoul Institute, Seoul, http://wish.welfare.seoul.kr/upload/data/_20150521002211392.pdf.

Ministry of Land, Infrastructure and Transport (MOLIT) (2017), "Housing Welfare Policy", presentation given to the OECD team on 20 September 2017, Seoul.

Ministry of Land, Infrastructure and Transport (MOLIT) (2016), *Korea Housing Survey 2016*.

New York City, Department of city Planning (2015), "Info Brief: NYC's Foreign-born, 200-2015", website, www1.nyc.gov/site/planning/data-maps/nyc-population/reports-presentations.page (accessed September, 2017)

OECD (2017a), "Divided Cities: Understanding Intra-urban Disparities", paper presented at the 33 WPTI, Paris, 5 December 2017.

OECD (2017b), Affordable Housing (database), www.oecd.org/els/family/HC1-2-Housing-costs-over-income.pdf (accessed August 17, 2017).

OECD (2017c), *International Migration Outlook 2017*, OECD Publishing, Paris, http://dx.doi.org/10.1787/migr_outlook-2017-en.

OECD (2017d), *OECD Environmental Performance Reviews: Korea 2017*, OECD Publishing, Paris, http://dx.doi.org/10.1787/9789264268265-en.

OECD (2017e), *Urban transport governance and inclusive development in Korea*, OECD Publishing, Paris, http://dx.doi.org/10.1787/9789264272637-en.

OECD (2016a), *Making Cities Work for All: Data and Actions for Inclusive Growth*, OECD Publishing, Paris, http://dx.doi.org/10.1787/9789264263260-en.

OECD (2016b), *OECD Economic Surveys: Korea 2016*, OECD Publishing, Paris, http://dx.doi.org/10.1787/eco_surveys-kor-2016-en.

OECD (2016c), *New York Proposal for Inclusive Growth in Cities*, www.oecd-inclusive.com/champion-mayors-doc/new-pork-proposal.pdf.

OECD (2016d), *Paris Action Plan for Inclusive Growth in Cities*, www.oecd-inclusive.com/champion-mayors-doc/paris-action-plan.pdf.

OECD (2016e) *OECD Regions at a Glance 2016,* OECD Publishing, Paris, http://dx.doi.org/10.1787/reg_glance-2016-en.

OECD (2016f), *Education Policy Outlook: Korea,* www.oecd.org/edu/Education-Policy-Outlook-Korea.pdf.

OECD (2015), *OECD Employment Outlook 2015*, OECD Publishing, Paris, http://dx.doi.org/10.1787/empl_outlook-2015-en.

OECD (2014a), *All On Board*, OECD Publishing, Paris, www.oecd.org/inclusive-growth/All-on-Board-Making-Inclusive-Growth-Happen.pdf.

OECD (2014b), *How's Life in Your Region? Measuring Regional and Local Well-being for Policy Making*, OECD Publishing, Paris, http://dx.doi.org/10.1787/9789264217416-en.

OECD (2014c), *Lessons from PISA for Korea*, OECD Publishing, Paris, http://dx.doi.org/10.1787/9789264190672-en.

OECD (2014d), *Education at a Glance 2014 – country note: Korea,* www.oecd.org/edu/Korea-EAG2014-Country-Note.pdf.

OECD (2013), *Strengthening Social Cohesion in Korea*, OECD Publishing, Paris, http://dx.doi.org/10.1787/9789264188945-en.

OECD (2012a), *Redefining "Urban": A New Way to Measure Metropolitan Areas*, OECD Publishing, Paris, http://dx.doi.org/10.1787/9789264174108-en.

OECD (2012b), *OECD Urban Policy Reviews: Korea 2012*, OECD Publishing, Paris, http://dx.doi.org/10.1787/9789264174153-en.

Seoul Metropolitan Government (2017), Answers provided to the OECD background questionnaire by Seoul Metropolitan Government.

Seoul Metropolitan Government (2016), *2015 Seoul Survey*, The Seoul Institute, Seoul.

Seoul Metropolitan Government and Seoul Institute (2016), *Seoul at a Glance 2016*, Hyunmum Group, Seoul, http://global.si.re.kr/content/seoul-glance-2016.

Shin, Young-jun (13 April 2011), "Inequality in Korean Education", The Korea Times, www.koreatimes.co.kr/www/news/special/2016/02/181_85160.html.

Son, J., et al. (2012), *The Impact of Heat Waves on Mortality in Seven Major Cities in Korea*, http://dx.doi.org/10.1289/ehp.1103759.

Tokyo Metropolitan Government (2016), "Tokyo Guidelines for the Promotion of Intercultural Cohesion", www.seikatubunka.metro.tokyo.jp/chiiki_tabunka/tabunka/tabunkasuishin/files/0000000755/shishin_all_eng.pdf.

WHO; World Health Organization (2011), *Seoul's challenges and achievements for an environmentally healthy urban transport system*, World Health Organization (Western Pacific Region), www.kdevelopedia.org/Resources/territorial-development/seouls-challenges-achievements-environmentally-sustainable-healthy-urbtransport-system--05201411200135419.do?fldIds=TP_TER%20TP_TER_TR#.

Yoon, M. S. (2016), *Features of elderly workers in Korea, and policy direction*, Seoul Institute, Seoul, www.dbpia.co.kr/Article/NODE06645554.

Chapter 2

Seoul is pioneering efforts to bridge climate action and inclusive growth

This chapter assesses the nexus between climate change adaptation, mitigation and inclusive growth in cities. It outlines the role of local governments in responding to the dual challenges of inequality and climate change, and identifies the synergies and trade-offs for policy makers to develop policy responses that address both issues in a mutually reinforcing way. The chapter analyses the climate challenge in Seoul, and the pioneering efforts of Seoul Metropolitan Government to ensure that strategies to tackle climate change – notably through its flagship initiative, The Promise of Seoul – are effective in engaging citizens and protecting the city's most vulnerable populations.

2.1. The nexus between climate change adaptation, mitigation and inclusive growth in cities

2.1.1. City governments are at the forefront of the response to inclusive growth and climate change

Income inequalities are more acute in cities relative to their respective national average and tend to be higher in larger cities (Chapter 1) (OECD, 2016). Inequalities go beyond income, affecting a range of dimensions that affect an individual's well-being, including access to quality affordable housing, transport, education, and jobs. They also have a strong spatial dimension: rich and poor residents tend to live in separate neighbourhoods. Such spatial segregation can reproduce disadvantages across generations (OECD, 2016). Although there are important differences across countries, local authorities have a hand in many policy areas that matter for inclusive growth, such as education, skills, housing and transport.

Public policies may explicitly or implicitly influence inclusive growth outcomes in cities. Some policies, such as social policies and programmes, welfare transfers or subsidies for transport and energy, have an explicit aim to reduce inequalities. Others, however, may not explicitly target a reduction in inequalities but can nonetheless influence inclusive growth outcomes due to their strong distributional effects. The potential effects of public policies on inclusive growth outcomes should be assessed *ex ante* to ensure that they are aligned with explicit inclusion objectives (Table 2.1).

Table 2.1. Public policies can explicitly or implicitly influence inclusive growth outcomes in cities

Explicit inclusive growth policies *Public policies explicitly aimed to reduce inequalities*	**Implicit inclusive growth policies** *Public policies that may not explicitly aim to reduce inequalities, but nevertheless have strong distributional outcomes*
Direct subsidies (energy subsidies, transport subsidies)	Tax policies
Social transfers	Education policies
Energy efficiency policies targeting poor households	Labour market policies
Social housing policies	Policies addressing the urban environment (land use, housing)
Welfare policies	Innovation policies (support to SMEs and start-ups)
	Infrastructure planning

Source: Authors' elaboration based on OECD (2015a); OECD (2016).

At the same time, city governments are also on the frontline to adapt to climate change and to protect vulnerable populations from its impacts. Cities are often first responders to natural disasters and the primary local planners of infrastructure (OECD, 2010). Many of the domains that fall under the jurisdiction of cities – land use planning, zoning, water provision, sanitation and drainage, housing construction, urban renovation, regulation, economic development, public health and emergency management, transport, environmental protection – are directly vulnerable to climate change impacts, but also represent opportunities to develop adaptive capacities and strategies (Hallegatte et al., 2016).

Cities can also play a major role in reducing greenhouse gas (GHG) emissions, a necessary condition to limit future damages from climate change. Cities account for more than half of the world's population (54.5% in 2016), consume 70% of the world's energy, and account for a roughly equivalent share of GHG emissions (OECD/Bloomberg

Philanthropies, 2014). They are major investors: subnational authorities accounted for 59% of public investment in 2015 in OECD countries and 40% worldwide (OECD/UCLG, 2016). Depending on the degree of autonomy in cities, many local decisions can directly affect the environment and GHG emissions, such as local authorities' regulation of transport, building construction, spatial planning, and economic development. Choices made in cities today about long-lived urban infrastructure will determine the extent and impact of climate change, our ability to achieve emission reductions and our capacity to adapt to changing circumstances. Table 2.2 provides an overview of the main policies that can influence climate outcomes at the city level, in terms of both explicit and implicit climate policies.

Table 2.2. Public policies can explicitly and implicitly influence climate outcomes in cities

Explicit climate mitigation policies *Public policies that aim to reduce GHG emissions*	**Implicit climate mitigation policies** *Public policies that do not explicitly aim to reduce GHG emissions but nevertheless have a strong impact on GHG emissions*
Carbon pricing, emission trading schemes	Tax policies, including property taxes
Targeted urban planning and development policies (e.g. compact cities, mixed use, transit-oriented development)	Transport and energy subsidies, parking fees
Transport planning, taxes and subsidies	Fiscal systems and intergovernmental transfers
Waste management (taxes and waste reduction)	Innovation policies
Energy efficiency initiatives (LED, energy infrastructure, building retrofitting)	Land use regulations, spatial planning
Environmental regulations (GHG emission limits)	Agricultural policies
Built environment and green space (rooftop solar panels, green roofs, parks and greenery, community gardens)	Energy policies
Water management (pricing, rainwater harvesting policies)	Innovation policies (tax breaks, R&D)

Source: Authors' elaboration based on OECD (2015b).

2.1.2. Climate change impacts are likely to further entrench structural inequalities in cities

Climate change is poised to exacerbate the effects of structural inequalities in cities. The impact of climate change on inequalities is still an emerging research field, and large uncertainties remain. However, inequalities and climate change impacts are mutually reinforcing: even if wealthier populations have more assets at risk, vulnerable populations are more exposed (IPCC, 2014). Moreover, cities with a poor environment or high climate risk will be less attractive and hence potentially less economically productive (OECD, 2010).

Three factors influence the vulnerability of low-income populations to climate change (UNDESA, 2016; Hallegatte et al., 2016):

- ***Increased exposure to climate risk and hazards***: low-income neighbourhoods are more likely to live in neighbourhoods that are more exposed to flood or landslides risks than more affluent areas, as the cost of housing often reflects exposure to risk.
- ***Higher susceptibility to damage***: disadvantaged groups are likely to live in homes that are not properly designed to face climate risks (e.g. poor insulation, underground flats, low-lying structures). For instance, low-income households may struggle to cope with heatwaves if they cannot afford air conditioning.

- ***Lower ability to recover***: low-income populations have more difficulty recovering from climate-related damages and losses, as they often lack access to social insurance systems and safety nets. They also may have limited access to public infrastructure (hospitals) to help them cope with a climate disaster.

Figure 2.1. Low-income populations are more vulnerable to climate hazards

The vicious cycle of climate change and inequalities

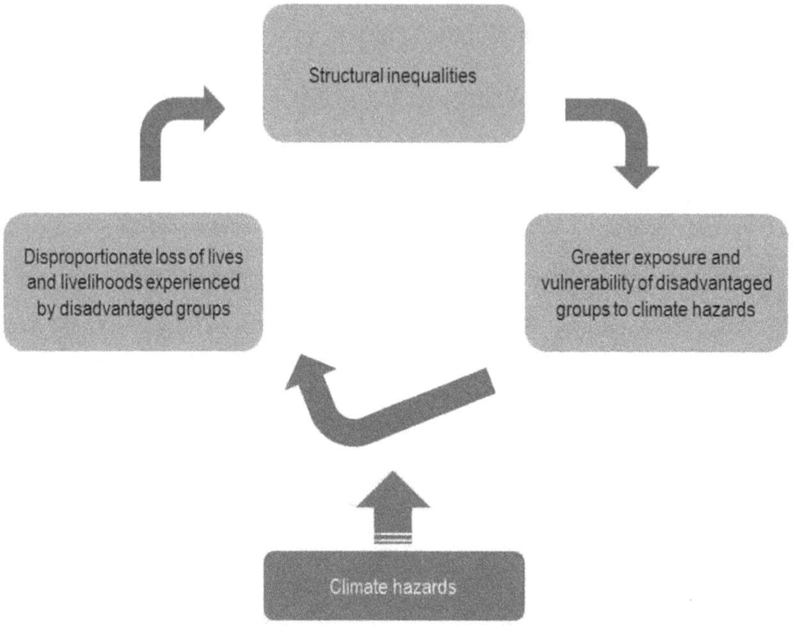

Source: Adapted from UNDESA (2016).

2.1.3. Climate adaptation and mitigation policies generate opportunities and trade-offs for inclusive growth in cities

National and local policies that aim to reduce GHG emissions and adapt to climate change have a range of economic and distributional consequences. Addressing climate change is a transformational agenda, as emissions from GHG, and particularly CO_2 from fossil fuels, are embedded in many human activities. Achieving the goal set by the Paris Agreement will require that global CO_2 emissions are drastically reduced to achieve net zero emissions by the second half of the 21st century. This calls for national and local policies that induce profound changes to infrastructure, technology and behaviours. For instance, core climate policies – such as those relating to energy, transport and carbon taxation; subsidy and pricing reforms; support for renewable and low-carbon energy; energy efficiency programmes; and transport planning and management – have the potential to affect household spending and the affordability of energy, transport services, and housing, particularly for low-income households.

Beyond core climate policies, policies *outside* the climate portfolio also influence climate and inclusive growth outcomes. For instance, local tax policies, by affecting the costs and benefits of land use, can have a significant impact on emissions and on housing affordability (OECD, 2017a). Other examples include parking fees, transport and energy subsidies, fiscal systems and intergovernmental transfers, land use regulations, spatial planning and water management.

Overall, there is a lack of empirical analysis of the distributional impacts of the low-carbon transition. Most studies focus on the impacts of climate policies on income and labour markets; less is known, however, about the impacts of climate policies on household welfare, mobility, health and social inclusion:

- ***Income***: Carbon pricing will have a regressive impact and risk disproportionately affecting low-income or energy-poor people in the absence of redistribution mechanisms (McInnes, 2017).
- ***Labour markets***: the low carbon transition will create jobs in a number of low-carbon economic sectors, but also lead to job destruction in carbon-intensive activities (OECD, 2017b). The low-carbon transition will strand carbon-intensive assets, activities and communities and create new and different needs in skills and training. OECD analysis shows that low-skilled workers are likely to account for the largest share of job destruction and job creation, while job turnover will be small for medium- and high-skilled workers, who will also benefit from new opportunities in green technology and innovation.

Climate policies and strategies thus present both threats and opportunities for more inclusive growth (Table 2.3).[1] For instance, increased investment in urban transport systems generally improves access to jobs for low-income populations. However, such investments can also lead to secondary impacts that are counterproductive in the long run: upgrading the public transport system may in some cases lead to gentrification and the displacement of lower income groups to lower quality, job-poor neighbourhoods, thereby reducing their access to jobs and services (OECD/ITF, 2017). Another example is congestion charges, which are generally understood to be regressive and risk disproportionately affecting low-income households living in the periphery where housing prices are cheaper. However, if the revenues of congestion charges are used to provide an affordable and reliable alternative (public transport), congestion charges could be leveraged to generate more equitable outcomes (OECD/ITF, 2017).

Table 2.3. Climate strategies and inclusive growth objectives: Opportunities and trade-offs

Climate policies or strategies	Impacts on inclusive growth outcomes		
	Dimensions of inclusive growth	Trade-offs	Opportunities
Carbon pricing	Income (energy affordability)	Higher energy and transport prices affecting low-income households	Revenues of carbon taxes could be invested in energy efficiency measures for low-income households
Energy efficiency programmes	Income (housing affordability, energy affordability)	Retrofitting programmes are expensive and new energy efficiency programmes are often more expensive than traditional social housing	If designed for low-income households, energy efficiency measures can improve the quality of housing and reduce energy bills
Transport demand management tools (congestion charges, restrictions on diesel and/or older vehicles)	Income (transport affordability) Access to jobs	Higher transport prices can restrict access to jobs and city centres to low-income populations Restrictions on older and/or diesel vehicles disproportionately affects poor households	The proceeds of the charge can be invested in better public transport systems to improve transport access, quality, safety and affordability
Phasing out of coal	Income Access to jobs	Ban on coal can strand low-skilled workers and communities in carbon-intensive industries	Retraining programmes can help higher-skilled workers transition to green jobs
Investment in transport-oriented development (TOD)	Income (housing affordability) Access to jobs and infrastructure Health	Risk of gentrification of neighbourhoods and exclusion/displacement of low-income populations if property values increase	Mass rapid transit systems, if well-designed, can integrate the periphery with the core of the city and better connect poor neighbourhoods with jobs, and improve air quality
Compact development, provisions and/or incentives to increase density	Access to jobs Health and well-being	Negative impact on the environment (e.g. heat island effect) Higher housing prices due to limited housing supply	Reduce sprawl, limit the need for carbon-intensive mobility, facilitate investment in public transport systems that benefit poor populations
Restrictive land-use planning in flood zones	Health Income (housing affordability)	Increased housing prices, limit new affordable housing	Decrease vulnerability to climate disasters
Provision of green spaces in low-income neighbourhoods for cooling effect	Income (housing affordability) Well-being, health Access to environmental services	Risk of gentrification and exclusion/displacement of low-income groups if property values increase	Better quality of life, health benefits for vulnerable populations in case of heat waves

Source: Author's elaboration, based on OECD (2017b).

2.1.4. Local governments have a key role to play in a just low-carbon transition

Climate change, if not mitigated, will increase inequalities and slow down growth.[2] This is because the number of extreme events will increase, often disproportionately affecting more vulnerable communities. OECD work has demonstrated that the cost of inaction is far higher than the cost of action, and that the *quality* of growth matters as much as the *level* of growth (OECD, 2017c).

The transition to a low-carbon economy must be inclusive. Given the high levels of inequality in many countries, public acceptability and the success of the transition towards a low-carbon future will depend on the fair and transparent distribution of the costs and benefits of this transition (OECD, 2017c). Workers in declining fossil-fuel intensive sectors will require support to transition to jobs in growing low-carbon sectors.

Resources will also be needed to help the poorest and most vulnerable cope with the climate impacts, which will become increasingly severe. Addressing these needs is a pre-requisite for a just and politically acceptable and sustainable transition.

Fortunately, climate, growth and inclusive growth objectives can be pursued in a mutually reinforcing way. Governments can achieve strong and inclusive economic growth in the near term, while reorienting economies towards low-emission development pathways with high resilience to the effects of climate change (OECD, 2017c). To achieve this, national and local governments alike need to implement a policy package of coherent climate, structural and fiscal policy reforms.

Local governments have a central role to play to ensure a just transition to a low-carbon economy. While sub-national governments do not often have the authority over energy and transport fuel taxes, they *do* in many countries have authority over land use, housing and transport policies. For instance, local governments have the opportunity to mitigate the regressive effects of taxes through the development of quality affordable transport alternatives (e.g. public transport) or campaigns to improve the energy efficiency of housing. They can also provide targeted support to small and medium-sized enterprises that have limited ability to provide on-site training, and particularly to identify skills in the local workforce that are transferable to fast-developing low-carbon sectors (Box 2.8 at the end of this Chapter) (OECD, 2017b).

2.2. The case of Seoul: Climate change impacts will likely further entrench structural inequalities

2.2.1. Seoul is particularly exposed to climate risks

The climate is already changing in Seoul, as inhabitants face rising temperatures and increased frequency of extreme weather events. It is also changing faster than in other parts of the globe: between 1911 and 2010, the average temperature increase in Korea was nearly double the global average. Seoul faces more warming than the national average: between 1975 and 2004, the annual mean temperature increased by 1.5 °C, compared to an increase of 0.6°C in rural and coastal areas of the country due to the urban heat island effect (Chung et al., 2004)[3]. Seoul has also seen an increased frequency in extreme weather events, such as torrential rains, floods and heatwaves. The primary damages from floods included flooded housing in low-lying areas; flooded underground facilities, roads and rivers; landslides on the hills of the city (there were 30 landslides in Seoul in 2010, and 50 in 2011) and casualties in river valleys (Kim, 2015).

Seoul's vulnerability to floods and heatwaves is driven by its intense urbanisation over the past decades that saw a rapid expansion of the city's built-up areas. Between 1975 and 2014, the built-up area of the metropolitan area has doubled (Figure 1.3). In the meantime, farmland decreased from more than 20% to 2% of the metropolitan area, while forested areas decreased slightly, from 28% to 24%. These trends have led to an increased vulnerability to floods and rising temperatures (Kim, 2015).

Climate change damages are expected to escalate in Seoul. While annual average temperature is currently around 13°C (2001-2010), it is expected to increase to 15.2°C between 2071 and 2100 (Seoul Metropolitan Government, 2012). This will lead to more extreme hot days and heat waves, increased water scarcity and drought, inland and groundwater floods and an increased risk of vector-borne diseases (Seoul Metropolitan Government, 2012). Heat wave-related deaths could double to about 1.5 deaths per

100 000 people over the period 2036-2040, compared to 0.7 deaths per 100 000 people over 2000-2010 (Seoul Metropolitan Government, 2015).

2.2.2. Climate change damages will disproportionately affect already vulnerable groups

While climate change damages can be spatially concentrated in cities, affecting low-income neighbourhoods more than high-income neighbourhoods, this does not appear to be the case in the city of Seoul, although more research on this would be useful. Some evidence suggests that the risk of floods and heatwaves in Seoul affects rich and poor neighbourhoods alike (Cho et al., 2012; Kim, 2017). There is no direct evidence that poor neighbourhoods are more exposed to climate change hazards: poor neighbourhoods have not necessarily been more exposed to flood risk in the past. The same is true for heat waves: the highest temperatures in Seoul are not necessarily evident in poor neighbourhoods (Seoul Metropolitan Government, n.d.).

However, climate change damages are likely to disproportionately affect already economically vulnerable groups in Seoul, as they are either more vulnerable to health impacts, or lack insurance and social safety nets to help them recover from damages. Vulnerable groups in Seoul include non-regular workers[4], low-income households as well as those with lower levels of education, women and the elderly. Over the period 2000-2010, mortality rates increased by 8.4% overall in Seoul during heat waves, compared to non-heat wave days – more than double the Korean average. Estimated risks were higher for women versus men, older versus younger residents, and those with no education versus some education (Son et al., 2012). Poorer households also have a limited capacity to recover from climate change damages. Non-regular workers in particular are vulnerable to climate shocks, as many are not covered by unemployment or property insurance should they lose their jobs or source of income in a climate disaster. Women and the elderly cumulate disadvantages, as they often belong to low-income groups: many women are non-regular workers, and half of the elderly people are poor (Chapter 1). The increased frequency of floods could also affect access to safe water and sanitation, and particularly the homeless (OECD, 2015c).

2.3. Seoul is at the forefront of cities' efforts to tackle climate change

2.3.1. The context for climate action in Seoul

Seoul's strong economic growth in recent decades has come with a rapid escalation of GHG emissions and a very high environmental cost. Seoul represents less than 10% of the nation's total emissions, which is small relative to the city's share of national population (around 20%) and GDP (Chapter 1). This is because most GHG emissions in Korea come from the manufacturing and energy sectors – representing 75% of emissions in 2015 – which are located outside the metropolitan area. The energy consumption of buildings and transport are the main challenge for Seoul, which together account for 91% of the city's total GHG emissions; their indirect emissions have more than doubled since 1990 (Compact of Mayors, 2017). In parallel, air pollution partly linked to fossil fuel combustion has also become a significant challenge in Seoul (Chapter 1).

Since 2009, the Korean national government has developed a strong policy framework, putting green growth and climate change as top priorities. The *National Green Growth Strategy* (2009-2050) structured the vision of a low-carbon, green-growth society around the three objectives of i) climate change mitigation and adaptation and energy independence; ii) creation of new engines of economic growth and improvement of quality of life; and iii) enhanced international outreach. The 2010 *Framework Act on Low Carbon, Green Growth* established a comprehensive institutional framework for its implementation (see also, Section 2.4.1).

Meanwhile, Seoul Metropolitan Government recognised early on the urgency of the climate challenge and the central role of cities in mitigating GHG emissions and adapting to a changing climate. In particular, 2011 was a key milestone for Seoul's energy and climate policies. Seoul's very low self-reliance rate on electricity – 2.95% – became a major source of concern after a large-scale nationwide blackout, partly due to a significant increase of 12% in the city's energy consumption between 2006 and 2011. In parallel, the Fukushima accident triggered strong opposition to nuclear power, which amounted to 30% of the country's electricity consumption and was the subject of ambitious expansion plans. Finally, as the city was strongly committed to fight against climate change, it realised the inconsistency of its energy mix, with renewable energy production representing only 1.5% of its total energy consumption (Seoul Metropolitan Government and Seoul Institute, 2014; OECD, 2017d).

2.3.2. Seoul's flagship mitigation strategy: One Less Nuclear Power Plant

In 2012, SMG launched its flagship energy policy, *One Less Nuclear Power Plant,* in response to concerns over the city's high dependence on energy imports, vulnerability to climate change impacts, and need to transition to a low-carbon economy. The comprehensive energy plan aimed to reduce the city's energy consumption by 2 million tons of oil equivalent (TOE) – equivalent to the amount of electricity produced by an average nuclear power plant in Korea – by the end of 2014 through the introduction of energy efficiency and conservation measures and the production of new and renewable energy. This target was exceeded in June 2014, six months ahead of schedule (Box 2.1).

The *One Less Nuclear Power Plant* programme encompassed six priority areas for climate action: i) expanded production of new and renewable energy through the provision of feed-in tariffs and low-interest loans; ii) a building retrofit programme (BRP) offering competitive loans to building owners and energy companies; iii) the establishment of an environmentally-friendly, high-efficiency transport system; iv) the creation of jobs in the energy industry; v) a shift to a low-energy, urban spatial structure, and vi) the promotion of a civic culture promoting energy conservation (namely through the eco-mileage programme, which mobilises households and businesses to reduce emissions through voluntary energy conservation measures).

While *One Less Nuclear Power Plant* was initially heavily focused on energy security, its second phase, the *Seoul Sustainable Energy Action Plan,* also integrated an important energy welfare dimension. The *Seoul Sustainable Energy Action Plan* went beyond energy and climate change to also address energy poverty, with citizen's participation at its core. It focused further on three core values:

- *Energy self-reliance,* with a goal of achieving an electricity self-reliance rate of 20% to limit exposure to power crises, by promoting mini-photovoltaic power stations on the roofs of school buildings, apartments and other structures to create local energy independent communities, known as energy self-sufficient villages (Box 2.3);
- *Energy sharing,* through the Energy Welfare Public Private Partnership, a globally recognised programme that helps low-income and marginalised populations reduce their energy consumption, while training and employing

disadvantaged job seekers to become energy auditors for low-income households; and

- *Energy participation,* through an open governance system to ensure the participation of all citizens in the entire energy policy making process, from policy planning to implementation (Box 2.1).

2.3.3. Seoul's adaptation strategy: Infrastructure and people

SMG has also introduced important adaptation measures. The city's *Ordinance on Tackling* Climate Change, enacted in 2008, included three articles on adaptation: Article 26 mandated adaptation measures responding to climate change; Article 27 required the establishment of a mechanism to research the impacts of climate change; and Article 28 prescribed a climate change impact and vulnerability evaluation test. In addition, following the adoption of the Framework Act on Low-carbon, Green Growth, local governments were required to develop local action plans as part of adaptation measures to climate change. SMG developed an adaptation strategy articulated around four main areas: i) disaster response and reduction of risks associated with extreme weather events (storms, floods, landslides); ii) protection from heat waves and air pollution; iii) water management to ensure clean water in the city; and iv) protection of forest and ecosystems to improve adaptability to climate change.

Box 2.1. Five year progress of *One Less Nuclear Power Plant* (2012-2017)

The main objective of the *One Less Nuclear Power Plant* initiative was to cut energy consumption by 2 million TOE (equivalent to the capacity of one nuclear power plant) by directly engaging citizens in energy-saving and renewable energy generation. This target was exceeded in June 2014, six months ahead of schedule. Beyond energy-saving benefits, the programme also provided a number of additional benefits, including awareness-raising among citizens.

Energy produced and saved: 3.66 million TOE of energy, or the output of 1.8 nuclear power plants (4 coal power plants) through energy-efficiency measures (e.g. LED lighting replacements) and the deployment of renewable energy.

Initiatives designed to boost citizen participation:

- *Eco-mileage programme*: 187 million members, which contributed to a reduction of 1.95 million tons of CO_2;
- *Energy self-sufficient villages*: 75 villages were created across the Seoul metropolitan area, with 22 additional villages in 2017 (see also, Box 2.3);
- *Energy Guardian Angels*: 10 000 primary and junior school students took the lead in energy saving actions at schools; and
- *Eco-driving Mileage*: 50 000 persons in 2016 (target to get to 250 000 in 2020).

Financing schemes:

- The *Seoul Energy Welfare Civic Fund*, run by citizens, reached KRW 755 million between June 2015 and December 2016; and
- *Emission Trading Scheme* (ETS) for GHG reductions in public buildings resulted in emissions allowances of KRW 13.5 billion.

Air quality, transport:

- 3 000 citizens participated in the debate on *air quality control solutions*; and
- 10 initiatives were launched for *clean air*, including energy retrofits and limitations on diesel vehicles; odd-even driving ban; green transport promotion zones (Low Emission Zone [LEZ]).

Recycling and resource conservation:

- *Seoul upcycling plaza*, an area dedicated to turning waste into new value-added goods, opened in September 2017, aimed to raise awareness on recycling; and
- The *rainwater re-use programme* was launched to develop rainwater recovery centres to water plants and gardens.

Health and safety:

- *Cooling shelters* for the elderly, to protect the vulnerable to heat waves from heat stroke: 3 000 in 2014, 3 251 in 2016 with the objective of 3 500 by 2020; and
- 100 000 *safety guards* to participate in emergency response, and prepare themselves and neighbours from disaster risk (40 000 in 2016).

Source: SMG (2017), Presentation from Boyoun HWANG, Assistant Mayor of Climate and Environment, SMG, Korea, at the Seoul Mayors' Forum on Climate Change 2017.

2.4. Towards inclusive climate policies in Seoul: Good practices and remaining challenges

Seoul has been at the forefront of cities' efforts to seize the opportunities created by low-carbon policies for more inclusive growth. While it is too early to measure the impact of policies on inclusiveness and climate outcomes, the following section takes stock of the good practices and remaining challenges, building on the OECD framework for *Policy Coherence for Sustainable Development* (Box 2.2). In particular, SMG has implemented a well-functioning people-centred adaptation strategy and has pioneered initiatives that seize opportunities to pursue climate and energy welfare objectives in a mutually reinforcing way. Further progress could be made to understand the trade-offs generated by climate mitigation policies, both within the city and the broader metropolitan area.

Box 2.2. The eight building blocks of policy coherence for development

To help countries achieve the Sustainable Development Goals (SDGs), the OECD has identified challenges and good institutional practices for enhancing policy coherence in SDG implementation. The *Policy Coherence for Sustainable Development Report 2017* introduces eight building blocks for policy coherence:

- **Political commitment**: Is there a clear statement at the highest political level backed by action plans?
- **Integrated approaches to implementation:** Have policy interlinkages, synergies and trade-offs been considered in sectoral strategies and proposals?
- **Long term perspectives**: Are there mechanisms in place to ensure sustained efforts beyond electoral cycles?
- **Policy effects**: Have the positive or negative impacts of policies on welfare of populations been identified, "here and now", but also "elsewhere" and "later"? Have the spillover effects of climate and inclusive growth policies been considered beyond the administrative boundaries, at the level of the functional area?
- **Policy and institutional coordination**: Are the coordination mechanisms located strategically to promote coherence and resolve potential conflicts of interests or inconsistencies between priorities and policies?
- **Aligning policies across levels of governments**: Are implementation responsibilities clearly divided and actions aligned across levels of government?
- **Stakeholder participation**: What are the mechanisms in place to ensure that stakeholder input feeds into decision-making processes?
- **Monitoring and reporting**: Are there mechanisms in place to monitor policy impacts and report to the public?

Source: OECD (2017e).

2.4.1. Key strengths of the Seoul approach to pursue climate and inclusive growth objectives in a mutually reinforcing way

Leadership and a strong political commitment at all levels of governments

Since 2009, the national government of Korea has developed a strong institutional framework for green growth and climate change, in response to Korea's high dependence on energy imports, its vulnerability to climate change impacts, and the need to transition to a less-resource intensive economic model. The *National Green Growth Strategy* (2009-2050) outlined a vision of a low-carbon, green-growth society (See Section 2.3.1). The 2010 *Framework Act on Low Carbon, Green Growth* established a comprehensive institutional framework for implementing the strategy and insisted on co-operation with subnational governments: all central and administrative agencies and local governments were required to develop annual green growth action plans. The national government developed five-year plans for green growth (2009-2013 and 2014-2018) to provide a roadmap for implementation.

While political priorities have shifted over the years, the new administration entering office in May 2017 has reconfirmed the country's commitment to tackle climate change under the Paris Agreement, which includes reducing GHG emissions by 37% of business-as-usual levels by 2030.

SMG has demonstrated a strong and consistent leadership on both climate change and inclusive growth. Seoul launched its flagship climate strategy, the *Promise of Seoul*, in 2015, followed by the *Ambitious City Promises* in October 2017, an initiative to enable and support cities in Indonesia, the Philippines and Vietnam to develop their own City Promise plans. In terms of inclusive growth, SMG introduced the *Economic Democratisation Agenda* as part of its efforts to level the playing field for small businesses and entrepreneurs (Chapter 3).

A long-term perspective with an integrated approach to implementation: The Promise of Seoul

In 2015, Seoul unveiled *The Promise of Seoul*, a comprehensive plan to address climate change mitigation, adaptation and citizen welfare in a mutually reinforcing way, while engaging citizens at all stages of the policy making process. The *Promise of Seoul* builds on the energy reduction efforts of *One Less Nuclear Power Plant*, but takes a holistic approach to the low-carbon transition by integrating other dimensions of the low-carbon transition, such as water, ecosystems, adaptation policies and health impacts. The plan provides an opportunity to consider the distributive impacts of adaptation and mitigation strategies beyond income, as well as other dimensions of inclusive growth, such as access to healthcare and clean water and protection from floods and climate impacts.

The *Promise of Seoul* combines GHG emissions reduction objectives along with adaptation efforts over the long term. The strategy aims to reduce GHG emissions by 25% by 2020 relative to 2005 levels, and by 40% by 2030. At the same time, it aims to create a healthy and safe city by strengthening climate adaptation through the expansion of disaster prevention facilities. The key objectives of the *Promise of Seoul* include:

- **Reducing risks and vulnerability to climate change**, including measures to protect citizens from disasters and infectious diseases. The adaptation strategy is organised around 5 key projects: the harvest and reuse of rainwater, the creation of small public parks and gardens in the city centre, the promotion of urban farming plots (the *roof gardening* programme), the training of 100 000 citizen safety-watchers to enhance the city's disaster response capability, and the desire to build a fast, effective response system against emerging infectious diseases.
- **Improving energy efficiency and reducing energy use,** with plans to save 5 million TOE by 2030 through energy efficiency and conservation, and to reduce emissions by 10 million tons of CO_2 by 2020 (approximately one ton of CO_2 per person). Renewable energy is expected to reach 14% of total consumption by 2030.
- **Reducing water consumption and improving water quality,** with a goal of reducing water consumption by 10 million tons by 2020.
- **Reducing private vehicle use and encouraging citizens to take public transport, walk and ride bicycles,** with objectives to increase the share of public transport usage to 66.5% by 2020. SMG also plans for a fourfold increase of bicycle lanes (to 2 000 km) and 250 pedestrian-only streets, up from 70, by 2030.
- **Increasing the supply of renewable energy** to 10% by 2020.
- **Improving solid waste management and scaling up recycling.**

With the *Promise of Seoul*, SMG has made an important shift in its adaptation strategy from an infrastructure-based approach towards a more people-centred approach. The people-centred approach focuses on flood preparedness and responsiveness, with a series of non-structural measures, such as flood alert systems and flood maps. Seoul's adaptation strategy is inclusive because it is tailored to the needs of citizens and local geographies, and it creates a sense of solidarity within neighbourhoods, notably with the creation of 100 000 citizen safety-watchers who are responsible for identifying vulnerable populations in the case of climate-related events, such as heat waves. Along these lines, SMG has identified specific needs of high-risk populations in the case of climate-related events – seniors, the homeless, poor people living in low-quality one-room housing – and has committed to develop tailored measures, such as the creation of cooling centres for vulnerable groups, measures to protect the homeless during extreme heat, and financial support for residents living in poor quality housing.

Innovative business models and financing schemes to deliver on climate and inclusive growth in a mutually reinforcing way

Citizen participation in the delivery of the *Promise of Seoul* builds on two innovative business models of the *One Less Nuclear Power Plant* programme, which was designed to deliver emissions reduction while raising awareness and creating a sense of solidarity within the city. The *Energy Welfare Public-Private Partnership Programme* reduces the overall energy bill of poor households, while decentralised energy systems, such as those implemented as part of the *Energy Self-sufficient Communities,* provide access to reliable energy sources for a broader share of the population, and increase resilience to heatwaves (Box 2.3).

Box 2.3. Innovative strategies to address climate change and energy poverty: Lessons from Seoul

Seoul has implemented two innovative policies that pursue climate and inclusive growth objectives in a mutually reinforcing way.

Energy Welfare Public-Private Partnership Programme

In 2015, Seoul launched the *Energy Welfare Public-Private Partnership Programme* to target vulnerable low-income families who would become even more at risk of energy poverty with the acceleration of climate change. The programme aims to increase the energy independence of energy-poor households by providing at-risk communities with home energy upgrades, including energy efficiency improvements, decentralised rooftop solar panels, and LED lights and mini-photovoltaic cells. It also supports disadvantaged job seekers through training and employment as energy consultants to assess energy performance of low-income households.

The programme operates with an innovative and sustainable financing method to ensure its long-term sustainability. This includes public funding from the city government for energy-efficiency building retrofits for low-income households, as well as the training of energy consultants. The programme also receives private funding from the *Energy Welfare Civic Fund*, into which citizens and businesses can make monetary and in-kind contributions. Contributions can come from savings earned through the *Eco-mileage programme* or the innovative "virtual power plant," through which 17 municipal buildings and 16 universities save electricity consumption during peak hours and donate profits towards the Fund.

Energy Self-sufficient Villages

Energy Self-sufficient Villages are community-led actions to reduce energy dependence on fossil fuels and nuclear energy, notably through energy efficiency measures and the deployment of renewable energy. Community efforts for energy self-sufficiency also include energy-related welfare activities, such as visits to senior households to check for energy leaks, or the use of the profits from "energy supermarkets" (which sell energy-saving products at affordable prices) to help members of the community in need. These initiatives help strengthen social linkages and raise awareness on the issue of energy poverty within communities.

Source: SMG (2012); SMG (2015); C40 (2016).

Stakeholder engagement and a comprehensive monitoring and reporting framework at all stages of policy making

Citizens' involvement and participation is at the core of development of The Promise of Seoul, with the aim to make this strategy the vision of the ten million citizens of Seoul. In the preparation phase, the Citizen Committee for Green Seoul (the city's representative body of eco-governance), the Citizen Commission of One Less Nuclear Power Plant and the Executive Committee of One Less Nuclear Power Plant called for visions and action plans to be drawn up to reduce GHG emissions. The Preparation Committee was formed, consisting of members of each committee as well as qualified experts with extensive research experiences from Seoul Institute. With citizen engagement identified as a central objective from the outset of the process, the Preparation Committee kept the public informed at each stage of preparation and consulted the public through major web portals, including the city government's official website. The city of Seoul aimed to ensure that governance centred on civil society. Civil groups as well as schools were proposed tasks for the *Promise of Seoul* and contributed to GHG emissions reduction (SMG, 2015).

Citizen participation has also been a key feature of the implementation of the *Promise of Seoul.* Citizen participation has been very high in a range of SMG initiatives: 187 million members for the *Eco-mileage programme*, 75 *Energy independent villages*, 10 000 primary and junior school students who took the lead in energy-saving actions at schools, 50 000 people in the *Eco-driving Mileage programme*); this also includes participation in financing schemes (*Citizen's welfare energy fund*) and the implementation of disaster risk management strategies (100 000 *citizen safety-watchers*).

SMG has also developed a comprehensive monitoring and reporting framework, with the implementation of indicators for each target outlined in the *Promise of Seoul*. Each year SMG releases an annual evaluation report of the *Promise of Seoul* and an evaluation of progress towards GHG reductions; the city has also committed to report annually on its progress towards global standards.

2.4.2. Remaining challenges of the Seoul approach to pursue climate and inclusive growth objectives in a mutually reinforcing way

Policy alignment: At the national level, the need to move away from an energy model based on coal and fossil fuel subsidies

Several major inconsistencies remain between climate objectives and energy policies at the national level. First, coal is still expected to remain a core part of the energy mix in Korea. Second, road transport continues to be supported through policy as the dominant form of mobility. Third, regulated energy prices remain among the lowest of OECD countries, and fail to reflect the cost of production and the environmental and social cost of electricity. These prices do not benefit energy-poor households, and by extension act as a barrier for increased penetration of renewable energy and energy-efficiency measures (Box 2.4).

There is also progress to be made at national level around inclusive growth policies, specifically in terms of the country's industrial structure and the structure of the labour market. The dual labour market leaves many low-income, non-regular workers with no access to unemployment insurance or pension scheme, increasing their vulnerability in the case of climate disasters; a number of social groups (women, youth, seniors) also face considerable disadvantages in the labour market (see Chapter 1 and Chapter 3). As OECD research has shown, more must be done to support low-skilled workers in the transition to the green economy, as they will be among those most negatively affected (Box 2.5).

Box 2.4. The reform of electricity prices in Korea

The Korean government has pursued a policy to keep electricity prices low to support industrial competitiveness and ensure affordable energy for households. This policy has, however, increased electricity demand and partially contributed to increased GHG emissions and tensions on the electricity supply, which led to major blackouts in 2011 (OECD, 2012). Low electricity prices are also a barrier to greater penetration of renewable energy – which accounted for less than 1% of electricity production in 2015 in Korea – and energy-efficiency measures (OECD, 2017d). Moreover, there is no evidence that such policies have benefited energy-poor households.

The national government has begun to increase electricity prices progressively since 2010 so that prices better reflect the costs associated with the system, but more reforms are needed to ensure that prices *also* reflect the social and environmental costs of electricity production, particularly for energy-intensive industries. The introduction of a tax on bituminous coal in electricity generation in 2014 is a step in this direction, but energy-intensive industries such as cement and steel are exempt from it. Other environmentally harmful fossil fuel subsidies need to be removed, such as the motor fuel subsidy paid to buses, taxis and liquefied petroleum gas (LPG) taxis since 2000 and extended in 2015 to diesel taxis.

Significant policy experience exists to address the regressive impacts of a rise in energy prices, and even transform these impacts into opportunities. Recycling tax revenues or savings through cash transfers or social tariffs can help limit the impact of carbon pricing policies on low-income groups. Policy makers could also design policies in a way that they provide economic, environmental and equity benefits, such as investing the proceeds of such taxes into the factors that underlie energy poverty and income inequalities, including more energy-efficient houses and appliances (OECD, 2012; 2017d; 2017c).

Source: OECD (2012); OECD (2017c); OECD (2017d).

The new national administration has indicated a commitment to address these issues. For instance, the government has announced the desire to replace coal-fired and nuclear power plants with renewable energy to ensure that 20% of the country's energy is renewable by 2030. To this end, the government has announced the near-term closure of 10 coal plants and allowed the operating license to expire as scheduled for Korea's oldest nuclear plant.

Box 2.5. Addressing the impacts of the low-carbon transition on low-skilled workers

The low carbon transition will create jobs in a number of low-carbon economic sectors, but also lead to job destruction in carbon-intensive activities. Low-skilled workers are likely to account for the largest share of job destruction and job creation (OECD, 2017b) while job turnover will be small for medium- and high-skilled workers, who will also benefit from new opportunities in green technology and innovation. In Seoul, the net effect of the low-carbon transition on jobs requires further research, but it is likely to further increase the duality of the labour market, between employees of chaebols with high skills and a good social protection and others in the work force, especially non-regular workers (Chapter 3).

The impact of the transition can be limited if labour markets are prepared. To maintain a high level of employment and a fair distribution of the transitional costs, three areas should receive specific attention (OECD, 2017b):

- *Supply-side policies,* with active labour market policies and skill development systems that can help facilitate a smooth reintegration of workers into employment;
- *Demand-side policies* to foster a competitive green sector through strong product market competition and moderate employment protection; and
- *Income support*, such as unemployment insurance and in-work benefits to ensure a fairer transition for workers.

Source: OECD (2012); OECD (2017b); OECD (2017c); OECD (2017d).

2.4.3. Recommendations: Towards greater integration of climate policies and inclusive growth outcomes

While SMG has developed a strong policy framework for more inclusive, low-carbon growth, there are several opportunities to further climate change and inclusive growth objectives in a mutually reinforcing way.

Collect data and develop indicators to understand the interactions of climate and inclusive growth outcomes, within and beyond the city's administrative boundaries

There is currently an information gap that if addressed would enable a more comprehensive assessment of the interactions between climate policies and inclusive growth policies in Seoul. It requires strengthening analytical capacity for policy coherence, and collecting appropriate data for the development of multi-dimensional indicators that would measure the social, environmental and economic impacts of climate change, transport, land-use and housing policies.

Such indicators would allow policy makers to consider systematically the effects of policies on people "here and now", but also "elsewhere" and "later" (OECD, 2017e), as outlined in the OECD *Policy Coherence for Sustainable Development Report 2017.*

It is essential to understand the consequences of climate policies on low-income citizens within the city boundaries, but also *outside* the city boundaries, within the functional urban area. For instance on transport, Seoul could develop indices of multi-modal location-based accessibility or integrated housing and transport affordability at the level of functional urban area. This would allow SMG to measure different scales and dimensions of accessibility within the broader functional urban area.

Mainstream climate and inclusive growth objectives in transport, land-use and urban planning

SMG has seized opportunities created by renewable energy and energy-efficiency policies to increase energy access and energy affordability for low-income households. Beyond the energy sector, however, more could be done to identify synergies and potential trade-offs in transport, land-use and urban planning – all areas essential to deliver low-carbon and inclusive growth. These sectors are often under the authority of local governments and have an important impact on both the carbon footprint of cities and several dimensions of inclusive growth, including the accessibility and affordability of transport and housing, and spatial segregation.

Along these lines, SMG could also consider including a systematic assessment of the potential impacts on climate outcomes and social exclusion in its analysis of proposed low-carbon transport and housing policies. Such an assessment could consider *ex ante* the potential impacts on inclusion spatially (will some neighbourhoods be more affected than others?) and across different groups of the population (will certain groups, such as the elderly, women, youth, migrant workers, non-regular workers, low-income populations, be disproportionally affected?) (OECD/ITF, 2017). This type of assessment could be useful in reviewing the existing congestion charge of the Namsan tunnels; congestion charges can be very efficient tools to limit air pollution and climate change in cities, but have a regressive impact that needs to be understood and mitigated to provide economic and social dividends and contribute to greater public acceptance (2.6).

2.6. Improving climate and inclusive growth outcomes: The congestion charge in Seoul

In 1996, a congestion charge was implemented in Namsan tunnels 1 and 3 (OECD, 2017d). While the congestion charge initially reduced vehicle volume and increased average speed through the tunnels, the rate has not been raised since its introduction due to public opposition, and its impact on congestion and GHG emission reductions has declined (OECD, 2017d). There is a need to increase the price and extend the coverage of the congestion charge. While such a reform could affect the affordability of transport for low-income households who live outside Seoul, it could also be an opportunity to recycle the revenues of the charge to invest in accessibility improvements, including affordable public transport alternatives for low-income groups.

Source: McInnes (2017).

Develop a long-term low-emission development strategy at the city level

The Paris Agreement recognised long-term, low-emission development strategies (LEDS) as an important policy tool to place short-term actions in the context of the long-term structural changes required to transition to a low-carbon, resilient economy by 2050. While developing climate strategies for 2020 and 2030 is an important first step, Seoul would also benefit from developing a longer term low-carbon strategy to 2050. The transformational changes required to achieve the objectives of the Paris Agreement will strand assets (e.g. inefficient buildings, bus fleets and vehicles) and communities (e.g. heavy industry or coal workers). LEDS can help cities identify the potential social and economic consequences of policy choices and develop compensation or training strategies to secure a just transition. In short, the development of a LED could enable SMG to balance the needs of current and future generations. New York City launched its *New York 2050 Strategy* along these lines (Box 2.7).

Box 2.7. OneNYC: A roadmap for an inclusive, sustainable and resilient New York City

OneNYC is a holistic roadmap for the City of New York to become a growing, just, sustainable and resilient city in the forthcoming decades. It is a long-term plan, which includes provisions to mitigate and adapt to climate change in a just manner.

New York City (NYC) was a frontrunner in mitigation even prior to the Paris Agreement. The City committed to reducing emissions by 80% by 2050 (known as 80 x 50) as well as an interim target of 40% by 2030 in September 2014. The City subsequently undertook an extensive analysis to identify the maximum potential for GHG reductions in energy, buildings, transportation, and waste. The City released their findings in September 2016, which found that OneNYC already puts the City on a track to significantly reduce GHG emissions. OneNYC sets specific targets for each of the following: i) significantly enhancing the energy efficiency of buildings, ii) replacing buildings' fossil fuel-based heating and hot water systems with renewable or high-efficiency electric systems, iii) transitioning towards a renewables-based electric grid, iv) reducing the number of miles driven in New York City while replacing remaining vehicles to zero-emissions vehicles, and v) achieving zero waste to landfills.

OneNYC also includes steps for adaptation. In particular, the roadmap includes measures and objectives to improve the city's response to extreme weather events like Hurricane Sandy, both in terms of continuing to deliver basic functions and services to all residents during such events, as well as eliminating long-term displacement from homes and jobs after such events. In the coming decades, NYC plans to upgrade private and public buildings to be more energy efficient and resilient to the impacts of climate change; adapt infrastructure, such as transport, telecommunications, water, and energy to withstand severe weather events; and strengthen coastal defences against flooding and sea level rise.

Moreover, the pursuit of these mitigation and adaptation goals is not at the expense of social justice and equity. OneNYC also intends to lift 800 000 New Yorkers out of poverty by 2025 by raising the minimum wage to USD 15, in addition to a number of education and retraining initiatives. OneNYC includes measures to reduce premature mortality amongst New Yorkers by 25% by ensuring access to medical and mental health services.

Source: New York City (2013); New York City (2014); New York City (2017).

Overcome administrative fragmentation and align policies across levels of government

There are also opportunities for SMG to improve coordination within the city administration (among different policy areas); with other neighbouring jurisdictions in the broader metropolitan area; and with other levels of government. Appropriate coordination mechanisms can foster horizontal coherence (synergies and interlinkages) as well as vertical coherence (from local to national to international) in the implementation of climate and inclusive growth policies (OECD, 2017e).

- *Within the SMG administration*: SMG has implemented a comprehensive framework to ensure that citizens, businesses and the administration are part of the governance process of the *Promise of Seoul* and develop a "whole-of-society" approach. However, significant fragmentation remains within the SMG administration, preventing the adoption of a "whole-of-local-government" approach to climate and inclusive growth. Improved coordination mechanisms would be beneficial, for instance between the department of climate change and the urban renewal unit, to better integrate climate and inclusive growth objectives across transport, housing and land use planning. One lever to facilitate cooperation could be to reflect climate and inclusive growth objectives in the incentive structure of the administration.
- *With other local governments in the metropolitan area*: While improvements to public transport systems in Seoul have been remarkable, more effective coordination at the metropolitan level could help improve social, environmental and economic outcomes across the population in the Capital Region. For instance, there is a significant gap in the modal share between the urban core and the periphery in Seoul: in 2010, public transport represented 52.4% of transport in Seoul but only 34% in neighbouring Incheon (OECD, 2017f). While Seoul and Incheon both have a sophisticated transport operation and information system that aims to improve user convenience, such systems operate within strict administrative boundaries under the rationale that they are entirely funded by local tax revenues (OECD, 2017f). To help achieve climate and inclusiveness outcomes in a more integrated way, efforts could be made to coordinate public transport policies at the scale of the Capital Region.
- *Across levels of government*: As mentioned, at national level, energy subsidies are a significant barrier to energy efficiency and renewable energy investments (OECD, 2012; OECD, 2017c; OECD, 2017d). Given that Korea has some of the lowest energy prices amongst OECD countries; the removal of fossil fuel subsidies is a necessary condition for efficient low-carbon policies in Seoul. Importantly, such a reform would not have to be at the expense of inclusive growth objectives. Indeed, there is significant policy experience demonstrating how to address the regressive impacts of increased energy prices (Box 2.5).

Another structural barrier to green and inclusive growth is the duality in the economy between chaebols and SMEs. The low-carbon transition requires innovation that is less likely to come from incumbent companies. Local policies need to help overcome the national economic bias favouring large conglomerates to allow the emergence of low-carbon innovative start-ups and companies (Chapter 3). Such a system is also a barrier to break the vicious circle that exists between climate change and inequalities: temporary workers in SMEs, women and the elderly have no access to insurance and social security systems will be less able to recover from climate damages. Expanding the social safety net to all would be the more inclusive adaptation strategy.

2.5. Bridging the climate and inclusive growth agendas: Good practices for city governments

This chapter has demonstrated that climate change and inclusive growth tend to be addressed through separate policy portfolios in cities, with limited attention paid to the trade-offs or synergies between these two areas. While efforts to address climate change and rising inequalities are not new in cities, less is known about how to effectively advance both agendas in a mutually reinforcing way. There is an emerging literature of good practices to help city governments address climate and inclusive growth concerns together (Box 2.8). It is nevertheless important to keep in mind that an effective joined-up strategy for climate and inclusive growth must be tailored to cities' specificities: the carbon intensity of its development, its vulnerability to climate impacts, its challenges in terms of inclusive growth and climate concerns, as well as its resources and capacities.

More importantly, all cities can adopt a common method and framework to pursue climate and inclusive growth objectives in a mutually reinforcing way. This includes: identifying priorities, understanding the potential synergies and trade-offs between climate and inclusive growth strategies, and selecting and designing efficient climate and inclusive growth strategies. Table 2.4 outlines preliminary policy guidance as a tool to guide mayors and city policy makers in aligning strategies for climate change and inclusive growth. It consists of a checklist of key questions to guide cities in: i) assessing the existing context and framework conditions and ii) considering dimensions of inclusion and environmental sustainability in the policy making process.

Box 2.8. How to make climate policies inclusive in cities? Examples of good practice

Cities can seize the opportunities created by low-carbon climate mitigation and adaptation policies to promote more inclusive outcomes, and mitigate potential trade-offs.

Mitigation

- Integrate inclusive growth objectives in low-carbon land-use and transport planning policies (e.g. affordability and accessibility criteria for transit-oriented city planning).
- Mainstream social diversity and climate objectives in urban regeneration programmes (e.g. eco-quartier Clichy Batignolles in Paris)
- Reinvest the proceeds of direct or indirect carbon pricing policies (e.g. congestion charges, ETS systems) into address addressing the roots of inequalities (e.g. invest in infrastructure to improve access to jobs and education; reduce the energy consumption of low-income households)
- Design tailored energy-efficiency programmes to low-income households, with tools to identify energy-poor households, and innovative financing arrangements programmes to totally cover fully the cost of retrofitting (e.g. Seoul energy welfare programme, that which fully finances totally building retrofit programmes)
- Seize the opportunity created by renewable energy investments to expand access to electricity access to households not connected to the grid, or to enhance the energy independence of energy- poor households (e.g. Seoul energy independent villages)

Adaptation

- Identify vulnerable populations throughout the city and the specific climate risks associated with these populations (e.g. Seoul's 100 000 citizen safety-watchers)
- Tailor emergency policy responses to the needs of targeted vulnerable populations (e.g. cooling centres for vulnerable populations in Seoul)
- Evaluate the impact of land-use regulation policies on vulnerable and low-income groups (e.g. the potential for higher housing prices that may result from restricted planning permissions)
- Extend the coverage of social safety nets and insurance programmes

Source: Authors' elaboration.

Table 2.4. Preliminary policy guidance: A Mayor's checklist to align strategies for climate change and inclusive growth

Diagnostic: Assessment of existing and framework conditions	Considerations for policy makers
1/ Develop a shared and long-term vision for low-carbon and inclusive growth	
• Are inclusiveness and climate outcome part of the city's overarching vision and strategy? ○ Has the city developed quantitative objectives for climate and inclusiveness? ○ Are inclusiveness concerns mainstreamed into climate change mitigation and adaptation plans? ○ Are inclusiveness and climate objectives mainstreamed into city plans, such as economic development, infrastructure and land-use planning? • Is there a process to consult and integrate public, private and civil society stakeholders in developing the city's strategy and vision? • Is there a process to identify populations, communities, activities and assets at risk of being stranded in a decarbonised future? (e.g. coal or energy intensive industries)	• How can green and inclusiveness objectives be better integrated into city plans, budgets and processes? • Which indicators can be developed to mutually assess the inclusiveness and climate mitigation benefits of policies? • How can the multiple benefits of climate policies be identified and communicated more broadly to the public? • How could the city develop an inclusive, long term low-emission development strategy?
2/ Design, reform and implement climate policies for inclusive growth	
Pricing	
• How is energy priced (taxes and subsidies)? ○ Are there taxes and pricing instruments that directly or indirectly value carbon (e.g. carbon taxes, congestion charges, parking fees, reforms of energy subsidies)? ○ What are the distributional impacts of those pricing instruments, and the impacts on vulnerable populations in terms of accessibility to jobs and public services? ○ Are alternative modes of transport (e.g. public transport, walking, cycling) adequate to ensure access to jobs and services? ○ Are there policies in place to mitigate the impacts of these policies? • Are energy and transport subsidies implemented with the objective of reducing inequalities and alleviating poverty? ○ Is the distributional effect of these policies evaluated (e.g. do they benefit low-income populations or the middle class?) ○ What are the environmental impacts of these subsidies, and are they consistent with long-term low-carbon objectives? • Do local subsidies exist to facilitate the penetration of renewable energy	• What compensation mechanisms could be directed to low-income households who may be affected by higher taxes on polluting vehicles or congestion charges? • How could the proceeds of congestion charges, parking fees or other environmental taxes be redistributed or reinvested in the development of more sustainable and inclusive activities (e.g. public transport)? • What is the scope to reinvest the proceeds of such taxes to address the drivers of energy poverty (e.g. retrofitting houses, providing energy with zero marginal cost)? • What policies could be implemented to facilitate the uptake of renewable energy in low-income households? • What measures can be put in place to pursue energy access and climate objectives in a mutually reinforcing way?

(e.g. subsidies for solar panels)? ○ Do these policies affect the overall price of energy at the city level? ○ Do these policies disproportionally affect low-income households?	
Regulations, standards and information policies	
• What regulations exist at city level to limit greenhouse gas emissions? To what extent do they affect vulnerable populations and inequality levels? ○ Land use regulations to limit urban sprawl or new development in areas exposed to climate damage ○ Energy efficiency standards for new buildings ○ Standards for eco-neighbourhoods ○ Restrictions for diesel and carbon-intensive cars in city centres, alternate traffic circulation • Does the city have green and inclusive procurement standards?	• How can inclusiveness and climate objectives be mainstreamed in the development of new housing? • How can alternatives to individual cars be made available and more affordable for low-income households? • How can inclusiveness and climate dimensions be factored into public procurement processes and decisions?
Measures to support energy efficiency and innovation	
• What is the share of the energy-poor in the city population? ○ What are the underlying sources of energy poverty (e.g. high levels of energy consumption of appliances or buildings)? • Has the city implemented policies or instruments to increase energy efficiency (e.g. subsidised loans and programmes to retrofit buildings and upgrade appliances)? ○ Do such supports reach low-income and vulnerable populations? • Are there specific policies dedicated to improve the energy efficiency of social and/or affordable housing? • Are there specific policies to support the emergence of innovative technologies, business models and financing instruments?	• What policies can help address energy poverty and improve the energy efficiency of buildings at the same time? • When it comes to support for innovation (social, technological, financial), have the potential impacts on climate change and environmental sustainability been considered? • Have the potential impacts on specific social groups and/or geographic areas within the city and metropolitan area been considered? • Have potential trade-offs and synergies been identified?
Adaptation strategies	
• Is there a climate risk assessment developed at the city level? ○ What populations are more at risk from climate change damages? ○ What are the socio-economic characteristics of populations located in disaster-prone areas? • What are the public health threats from air pollution? ○ Are particularly areas of the city more affected? • To what extent does the welfare system protect vulnerable and low-income populations? ○ Do such populations have access to insurance to protect their assets?	• To what extent is new proposed infrastructure low-carbon and resilient? ○ What level of risk is new infrastructure protected against? • What adaptation strategies can be developed to address climate change risks for vulnerable populations? • How can climate risk assessments be integrated into infrastructure and land-use planning? • How can information systems be used to learn from and react to changing circumstances, including to climate

	change disasters?
3/ Mainstream climate and inclusiveness concerns in housing, land-use, transport and infrastructure planning	
• What are the current infrastructure gaps in the city and broader metropolitan area? ○ To what extent is the existing infrastructure low-carbon? • Are public transport systems affordable? Accessible? Low-carbon? ○ Is accessibility to public transport linked to socio-economic factors? • Is housing affordability a challenge? For whom? ○ Is gentrification and/or displacement a threat in some neighbourhoods? ○ In the case of residential segregation, is there evidence that it contributes to unequal access to jobs, public services or education opportunities?	• To what extent will new infrastructure investments improve the accessibility, affordability and/or quality of public services? ○ To what extent will these dimensions improve (or deteriorate) for different social groups, firms and geographic areas? • To what extent is the infrastructure screening process multi-dimensional, taking into account economic, environmental, social, and cultural criteria *ex ante*? ○ Have the potential impacts on climate change and environmental sustainability been considered? On specific social groups, businesses and geographic areas? ○ Have potential trade-offs and synergies been identified? • To what extent do neighbourhood improvement strategies include measures to address the threat of gentrification and displacement? ○ To what extent do urban regeneration programmes integrate climate challenges at the outset? • Are information and communication technologies integrated into infrastructure planning? ○ Are information systems used to engage effectively with communities and stakeholders to improve citizen participation?
4/ Ensure that green jobs benefit all	
• What are the strengths and challenges of the local workforce? ○ What is the share of high-skilled vs. low-skilled workers in the city? ○ What share of the population is unemployed or underemployed? ○ Are specific social groups more affected than others? • What share of firms and workers are employed in sectors linked to the fossil-fuel industry? • What share of firms and workers are employed in the Environmental Goods and Services Sector?	• Have the potential impacts of a low-carbon future on workers of different skills levels been taken into account? ○ Have mitigating measures been put into place to address the challenge of stranded communities (e.g. communities relying on fossil fuel-intensive activities)? ○ What opportunities exist to facilitate the retraining of workers? ○ What skills could be transferred to a low-carbon economy?

	• Are there active labour market policies and skill development systems in place to facilitate a smooth reskilling and reintegration of workers? o Are such policies sufficiently flexible to be adapted to local characteristics, and can the city influence their implementation?
5/ Promote responsible business conduct and innovation for green and inclusive growth	
• Is the policy framework at higher levels of government conducive to the emergence of green innovation and technologies? To innovative business models? • Is the overall policy framework conducive to the emergence of new businesses? • To what extent are firms of all sizes able to contribute to and benefit from innovation and new technological advances? • To what extent are specific social groups and/or geographic areas able to contribute to and benefit from digitalisation and new technological advances? o To what extent are such innovations detrimental to specific groups or geographic areas?	• What information programmes and public awareness campaigns could be designed to encourage low-carbon and inclusive behaviours from firms (e.g. voluntary programmes)? • How can policies better support the adoption of sustainable practices by SMEs? • How can local initiatives be expanded to strengthen SME access to technology, innovation and knowledge networks? • To what extent do regulations favour or hamper the emergence of innovative business models? • What strategies can help to ensure that innovations to address climate change do not further entrench inequalities (e.g. labour market impacts of the sharing economy – the "uberisation" of the economy)?
6/ Align policies and develop capacities at all levels of governments	
At city level	
• What strategic framework(s) exist to guide public policies for climate change? o For inclusive growth? o Do these strategies explicitly link to one another? • To what extent are climate and inclusion objectives mainstreamed across the many departments and public policy streams? o Are these objectives reflected in the incentive structure of the administration? • To what extent do *other* policies or programmes (e.g. those outside the realm of climate and social policy) affect inclusiveness and climate change outcomes? • How does the city's policy framework align with objectives at higher levels of government?	• What processes can support a whole-of-city view to ensure that efforts to promote climate change and inclusive growth are mutually reinforcing? • What processes can ensure that policies and initiatives that do not explicitly address climate change or inclusiveness nonetheless support – or at least do not undermine – climate and inclusiveness objectives? • How could new partnerships between the city administration and other public authorities, firms, business associations, social enterprises, residents and civil society be developed to address climate change and advance inclusive growth?

• Who are the traditional partners of the city administration to deliver on climate change and inclusive growth (other public authorities, neighbouring jurisdictions, firms of all sizes, social enterprises, residents, civil society)? ○ To what extent are citizens engaged in all phases of the policy making process and implementation phases? ○ Do residents have any role in decisions around the public budget or public investment? • How much of the city's budget relies on royalties or taxes from fossil fuel incentives/activities, or activities favouring urban sprawl?	
At metropolitan level	
• What is the relevant scale of analysis for inclusiveness and climate outcomes? • What are the social and climate consequences of city-level policies on the broader metropolitan area?	• To what extent have the potential impacts on neighbouring jurisdictions and the wider metropolitan area been considered? • To what extent have transport and land-use planning decisions been integrated at the level of the metropolitan area? • To what extent have the social and climate impacts of city-level policies been measured at the level of the metropolitan area?
At national level	
• What is the national framework that governs the "fiscal space" of the city government? ○ How much of the city's budget is dependent on transfers from other levels of government? ○ How much revenue-raising capacity does the city government have? ○ Is the city able to raise revenue on international markets?	• What policies at national level may contradict or act against climate and inclusiveness outcomes?

Source: Author's elaboration.

Notes

[1] The C40 Cities Climate Leadership Group, through its Inclusive Climate Action initiative, is undertaking a mapping of the impacts that can result from a range of policy domains.

[2] http://news.berkeley.edu/2017/06/29/new-study-maps-out-dramatic-costs-of-unmitigated-climate-change-in-u-s/.

[3] As dark surfaces absorb more solar radiation, the concentration of roads and buildings in urban areas results in warmer temperatures in metropolitan areas relative to suburban and rural areas.

[4] As mentioned in Chapter 1, non-regular workers have a fixed-term contract with generally lower salaries and poor social coverage.

References

C40 (2016), "Cities100: Seoul - Public-Private Partnership Prevents Energy Poverty", C40 Case Study Library, www.c40.org/case_studies/cities100-seoul-public-private-partnership-prevents-energy-poverty (accessed September, 2017).

Cho, G.W., S.H. Chung, and H.M. Lee (2012), *Study on Quantifying Risk of the Effects of Climate Change,* Korea Environment Institute, Seoul.

Chung. Y.S., M.B. Yoon, and H.S. Kim (2004), "On Climate Variations and Changes Observed in South Korea," *Climatic Change,* Vol. 66, Springer, New York, pp. 151-161, www.springerlink.com/content/q152256357827858/.

Compact of Mayors (2017), "Data for Seoul", website, www.compactofmayors.org/cities/seoul.

Hallegatte et al. (2016), *Shock Waves: Managing the Impacts of Climate Change on Poverty*, World Bank, Washington D.C., http://hdl.handle.net/10986/22787.

IPCC; Intergovernmental Panel on Climate Change (2014), *Climate Change 2014: Impacts, Adaptation, and Vulnerability. Part A: Global and Sectoral Aspects - Contribution of Working Group II to the Fifth Assessment Report of the IPCC*, Cambridge University Press, Cambridge and New York, http://dx.doi.org/10.1017/CBO9781107415379.

Kim, W.J. (2017), *Roof Gardening Support Project for Private Buildings*, The Seoul Institute, Seoul.

Kim, Y.R (2015), *Seoul's flood control policy*, The Seoul Institute, Seoul.

McInnes, G. (2017), *Understanding the Distributional and Household Effects of the Low-carbon Transition in G20 Countries*, www.oecd.org/environment/cc/g20-climate/collapsecontents/McInnes-distributional-and-household-effects-low-carbon-transition.pdf.

New York City (2017), *Aligning New York City with the Paris Climate Agreement,* www1.nyc.gov/assets/sustainability/downloads/pdf/publications/1point5-AligningNYCwithParisAgrmtFORWEB.pdf.

New York City (2014), *New York City's Roadmap to 80 X 50,* http://www1.nyc.gov/assets/sustainability/downloads/pdf/publications/New%20York%20City's%20Roadmap%20to%2080%20x%2050_20160926_FOR%20WEB.pdf.

New York City (2013), *One New York – The Plan for a Strong and Just City,* www.nyc.gov/html/onenyc/downloads/pdf/publications/OneNYC.pdf.

OECD (2017a), *The Governance of Land Use in OECD Countries: Policy Analysis and Recommendations*, OECD Publishing, Paris, http://dx.doi.org/10.1787/9789264268609-en.

OECD (2017b), *Impacts of Green Growth Policies on Labour Markets and Wage Income Distribution*, OECD Publishing, Paris.

OECD (2017c), *Investing in Climate, Investing in Growth*, OECD Publishing, Paris, http://dx.doi.org/10.1787/9789264273528-en.

OECD (2017d), *OECD Environmental Performance Reviews: Korea 2017*, OECD Publishing, Paris, http://dx.doi.org/10.1787/9789264268265-en.

OECD (2017e), *Policy Coherence for Sustainable Development 2017: Eradicating Poverty and Promoting Prosperity: Building blocks for coherent implementation of the Sustainable Development Goals,* OECD Publishing, Paris, http://dx.doi.org/10.1787/9789264272576-4-en.

OECD (2017f), *Urban transport governance and inclusive development in Korea*, OECD Publishing, Paris, http://dx.doi.org/10.1787/9789264272637-en.

OECD (2016), *Making Cities Work for All: Data and Actions for Inclusive Growth,* OECD Publishing, Paris, http://dx.doi.org/10.1787/9789264263260-en.

OECD (2015a), *OECD Employment Outlook 2015*, OECD Publishing, Paris, http://dx.doi.org/10.1787/empl_outlook-2015-en.

OECD (2015b), *Aligning Policies for the Transition to a Low-carbon Economy*, OECD Publishing, Paris, http://dx.doi.org/10.1787/9789264233294-en.

OECD (2015c), *Water and Cities: Ensuring Sustainable Futures*, OECD Publishing, Paris, http://dx.doi.org/10.1787/22245081.

OECD (2012), *OECD Urban Policy Reviews: Korea 2012*, OECD Publishing, Paris, http://dx.doi.org/10.1787/9789264174153-en.

OECD (2010), *Cities and Climate Change*, OECD Publishing, Paris, http://dx.doi.org/10.1787/9789264091375-en.

OECD (2007), *OECD Framework for the Evaluation of SME and Entrepreneurship Policies and Programmes,* OECD Publishing, Paris, http://dx.doi.org/10.1787/9789264040090-en.

OECD/Bloomberg Philanthropies (2014), *Cities and Climate Change: National Governments Enabling Local Action*, www.oecd.org/environment/cc/Cities-and-climate-change-2014-Policy-Perspectives-Final-web.pdf.

OECD/ITF (2017), *Income Inequalities, Social Inclusion and Mobility*, International Transport Forum, Paris, www.itf-oecd.org/income-inequality-social-inclusion-mobility.

OECD/UCLG (2016), *Subnational governments around the world: Structure and finance*, www.oecd.org/regional/regional-policy/Subnational-Governments-Around-the-World-%20Part-I.pdf.

Seoul Metropolitan Government (2017), Presentation from Boyoun HWANG, Assistant Mayor of Climate and Environment, at the Seoul Mayors Forum on Climate Change 2017 in Seoul Korea, October 20, 2017.

Seoul Metropolitan Government (2015), *The Promise of Seoul,* http://worldcongress2015.iclei.org/wp-content/uploads/2015/04/promise-of-SEOUL_short-version.pdf.

Seoul Metropolitan Government and Seoul Institute (2014), *One Less Nuclear Power Plant,* www.ieac.info/IMG/pdf/20140914olnpp2-lr.pdf.

Seoul Metropolitan Government (2012), *Detailed Action Plans for Adaptation Measures to Climate Change,* www.globalcovenantofmayors.org/wp-content/uploads/2015/06/2.-SMG_Summary_Detailed-Implementation-Plans-to-adapt-to-Climate-Change_EN-1.pdf.

Seoul Metropolitan Government (n.d), "서울특별시 대기환경정보 - 기후지도" [SMG Climate and Environment Information - Climate Map], webpage, http://cleanair.seoul.go.kr/climate_map.htm?method=temp (accessed July 2017).

Son, J., et al. (2012), *The Impact of Heat Waves on Mortality in Seven Major Cities in Korea,* http://dx.doi.org/10.1289/ehp.1103759.

UNDESA (2016), *World Economic and Social Survey 2016: Climate Change Resilience – An Opportunity for Reducing Inequalities.*

Chapter 3

Strengthening SMEs and entrepreneurship through the *Economic Democratisation Agenda*

This chapter analyses the contributions of small and medium-sized enterprises (SMEs) and entrepreneurship towards more inclusive growth in Seoul. It identifies the main challenges facing SMEs and entrepreneurs in Seoul. It then takes a closer look at how the city's Economic Democratisation Agenda, introduced by Seoul Metropolitan Government in 2016, is addressing the obstacles facing SMEs and entrepreneurs, as well as measures that could further strengthen its impact.

3.1. SMEs and entrepreneurship are important vehicles to more inclusive growth in Seoul

A diverse, innovative and competitive small and medium-sized enterprises (SMEs) sector is generally recognised as essential for economic growth. Across OECD countries, SMEs represent more than 95% of firms, provide the majority of training opportunities, account for 60% of total employment, and are responsible for the majority of new jobs. They also generate 50 to 60% of value-added on average (OECD, 2017a). An inclusive SME sector is one that contributes to economic growth and competitiveness, whilst ensuring that economic benefits are widely shared among the population. Entrepreneurship, which is the creation of productive new businesses by individuals, is key to ensuring that new ideas generate innovations and advance economic development. Inclusive entrepreneurship aims to ensure that all parts of the population have an equal opportunity to start and run a business, independent of their age, gender or education.

Sustainable business creation and small business development will play a major role in driving future economic development and social inclusion in Seoul. SMEs are the dominant source of employment in Seoul; SMEs and entrepreneurship also make critical contributions to wages and household incomes, and help drive innovation and economic growth. However, SMEs and entrepreneurs tend to be more sensitive than large businesses to shocks in the business environment and changes in economic conditions, and often face lower job quality. This calls for policy action to create a thriving and inclusive SME sector. Getting policies right could have a substantial impact on Seoul's workforce and the economy.

3.1.1. Structure of businesses in Seoul

Given the strong practice of business ownership and self-employment in Seoul, entrepreneurship – if centred around inclusive growth – has the potential to address economic exclusion. The growth in number of SMEs and microbusinesses has been continuous over the last decade with an annual growth rate of 1.49% and 1.81% respectively from 2007-14. Meanwhile, the growth of large firms was high in 2008 and 2010 before becoming negative in 2013 and 2014, with slightly fewer companies being registered in Seoul than in the years before (Box 3.1 and Table 3.1).

Box 3.1. The SME definition in Korea

Article 2 of the Framework Act on SMEs and the related Enforcement Decree defines a micro, small, and medium enterprise in Korea as an establishment with less than 300 regular employees or paid-in-capital less than or equal to KRW 8 billion (about USD 8 million). This definition is used by the Bank of Korea (BOK) and the FSS (Financial Supervisory Service). However, criteria differ by sector (Table 3.1Table 3.1).

Table 3.1. Definition of SMEs in Korea, by sector

Sector	Medium enterprises		Small Business	Micro-enterprises
	Number of Workers	Capital & Sales	Number of Workers	
Manufacturing	Less than 300	Capital worth USD 8M or less	Less than 50	Less than 10
Mining, construction and transportation	Less than 300	Capital worth USD 3m or less	Less than 50	Less than 10
Large general retail stores, hotel, recreational condominium operation, communications, information processing and other computer-related industries, engineering service, hospital and broadcasting	Less than 300	Sales worth USD 30m or less	Less than 10	Less than 5
Seed and seedling production, fishing, electrical, gas and waterworks, medical and orthopaedic products, wholesales, fuel and related products wholesales, mail order sale, door-to-door sale, tour agency, warehouses and transportation-related service, professional, science and technology service, business support service, movie, amusement and theme park operation	Less than 200	Sales worth USD 20m or less	Less than 10	Less than 5
Wholesale and product intermediation, machinery equipment rent for industrial use, R&D for natural science, public performance, news provision, botanical garden, zoo and natural parks, waste water treatment, waste disposal and cleaning related service	Less than 100	Sales worth USD 10m or less	Less than 10	Less than 5
Other sectors	Less than 50	Sales worth USD 5m or less	Less than 10	Less than 5

Note: General Criteria (Article 2 of Framework Act on SMEs and Article 3 of Enforcement Decree of the Act). For micro-enterprises, Article 2 of the Act of Special Measures on Assisting Small Business and Micro-enterprises applies.
Source: OECD (2017b), *Financing SMEs and Entrepreneurs 2017*.

The SME sector in Seoul is comprised primarily of small and micro firms mostly situated in sectors with lower value-added, which points toward a challenge in its capacity to scale up and a predisposition to lower productivity industries. Seoul's SMEs sector is dominated by micro-businesses, that is, businesses with less than 10 employees, which account for 91.3% of the business population in Seoul and in 2014 employed 35% of the workforce. On the other hand, small and medium-sized businesses (10-300 employees) make up only about 8% of all businesses, with the distribution skewed toward smaller businesses, and employ about 44% of workforce. Large businesses represent just 1.6% of all firms, but employ about 21% of all workers in Seoul (Table 3.2).

Table 3.2. Employment size structure of Seoul enterprises, 2014

Number of companies and number of employees by firm size

	1-4	5-9	10-19	20-49	50-99	100-299	300-499	500 - 999	More than 1 000	Total
Number of companies	650 125	99 353	39 099	20 111	6 572	4 007	675	441	275	820 658
Percentage (%)	79.2	12.1	4.8	2.5	0.8	0.5	0.1	0.1	0.03	100.0
Number of employees	1 176 347	632 631	511 697	593 613	453 779	645 550	258 400	299 510	537 301	5 108 828
Percentage (%)	23.0	12.4	10.0	11.6	8.9	12.6	5.1	5.9	10.5	100.0

Source: Seoul Statistics.

There is a large dominance of SMEs in services relative to manufacturing. About 30% of self-employed and SMEs can be found in the wholesale and retail sector, followed by accommodation and food (16%) (Figure 3.1). Nevertheless, Korea's strong export-led growth over the past decades has shifted a great deal of capital and talent from services towards large manufacturing companies, thereby further weakening productivity in the SME-dominated service sector (see Section 3.2).

Figure 3.1. Distribution of SMEs in Seoul by sector, 2014

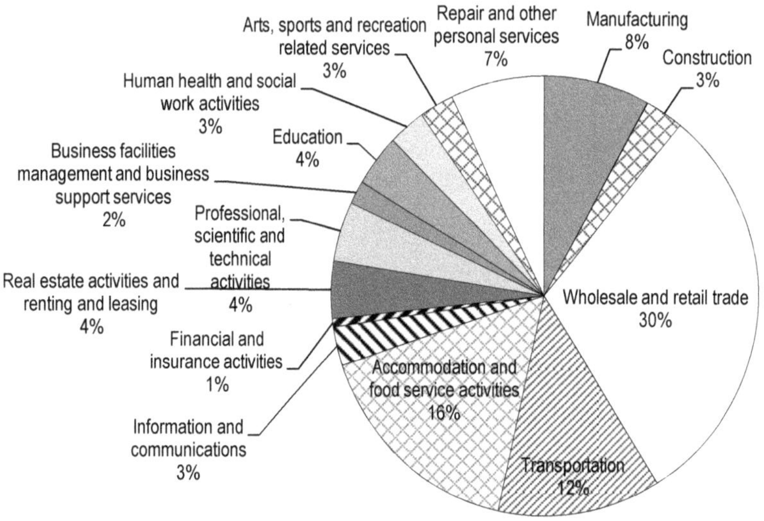

Source: Statistics Korea.

Female business ownership is lower than male business ownership in Seoul. Around 57% of all businesses in Seoul are owned by men, compared to 43% by women. Female business ownership is largely present in the service sector, such as accommodation and food services, as well as education. Low rates of female owned-businesses in higher value-added and more knowledge-intensive industries indicate additional barriers women may face in business creation and self-employment.

3.1.2. Business demography

Business demography indicators – that is, business entry (birth) and exit (death) rates – provide an overview of entrepreneurial dynamics and are key indicators of job creation. The OECD finds, for example, that young firms (5 years old or less) accounted for on average 17% of employment over the past decade, but generated nearly half of all new jobs across a range of OECD countries (Criscuolo et al, 2014). Moreover, across OECD countries, an increase in the share of young firms (aged 6 years or less) relative to old firms (aged 12 years or more) is associated with an increase in multifactor productivity (MFP) growth, which can be primarily attributed to start-ups (aged 3 years or less) (OECD, 2015a).

In Seoul, the employer enterprise birth rate and death rate were quite high (14.6% and 13.1%, respectively) between 2007 and 2014 (Table 3.3). These figures are higher than for the rest of Korea, which had a firm birth rate of 9% and a death rate of below 5% in 2014 (OECD, 2017c) and also point toward a relatively high churn rate of 27.7%, which is equivalent to the sum of birth and death rates. The churn rate provides a measure of how frequently firms close and new firms are created, and reflect a country's degree of entrepreneurial dynamism. The average churn rate in the OECD has been around 20% (OECD, 2017c).

Table 3.3. Employer enterprise birth and death rates in Seoul, 2007-2014

Enterprise births and deaths as share of the total active business population per year

	Enterprise birth rate (%)	Enterprise death rate (%)
2007	17.6	13.5
2010	14.5	12.4
2012	13.4	12.9
2014	14.1	14.5

Source: Statistics Korea.

Churn rates can be a sign of a dynamic business sector, but they can also imply that many new businesses fail to sustain in the market. Low survival rates of newly created firms can be a disincentive for new entrepreneurs to enter the market and for investors to provide financial support to new firms. Observing post-entry performance of firms is therefore just as important as looking at their birth rates. OECD (2015b) finds that the survival rate of new enterprises in the OECD is equal to just above 60% after three years from entry. Businesses in Seoul display lower survival rates than the OECD average, with a three years survival rate of 38.8% in 2014 (however the survival rate in Seoul is higher than the Korean average of 40.1%) (Figure 3.2). This implies that a fairly large share of companies exit the market. While high entrepreneurial dynamism is in principle associated with net job creation, it is also important that the business environment facilitates long-term growth and innovation of companies.

Figure 3.2. Three-year survival rate of new enterprises in Seoul and Korea (2010-2014)

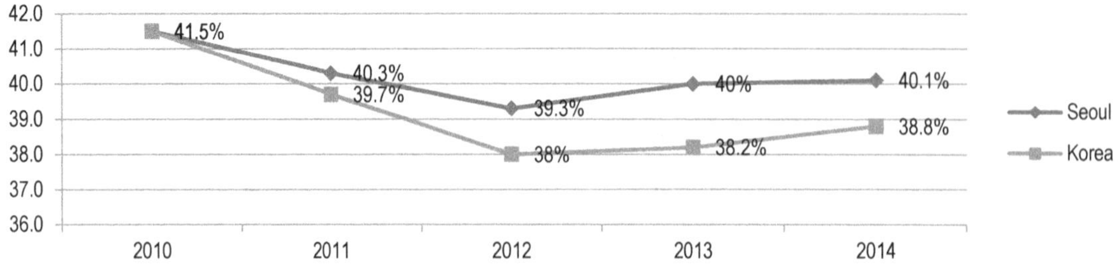

Source: Statistics Korea.

High-growth enterprises

High-growth enterprises – firms which grow rapidly over a short period of time – are a major source of job creation. The OECD found that although high-growth firms represent only between 3.2% and 6.4% of the total enterprise stock in several countries, they account for between 40% and 64% of all new jobs in these countries (Bravo-Biosca et al., 2013). High-growth enterprises also contribute to the process of creative destruction and often generate spill-overs that can be harnessed by other firms (Bravo-Biosca et al., 2013; Mason and Brown, 2014).

Figure 3.3 shows that the rate of high-growth firms as a percentage of the total business population is relatively low in Seoul when measured by employees and turnover, and has decreased from 3% in 2009 to 2.3% in 2015. The share of high-growth enterprises is however significantly higher when measured by turnover only with 8.6% in 2015, implying that higher profits and firm growth do not necessarily translate into employment growth in firms.

Figure 3.3. High-Growth Enterprises in Seoul, 2009-2015

Share of high-growth enterprises compared to the total business population

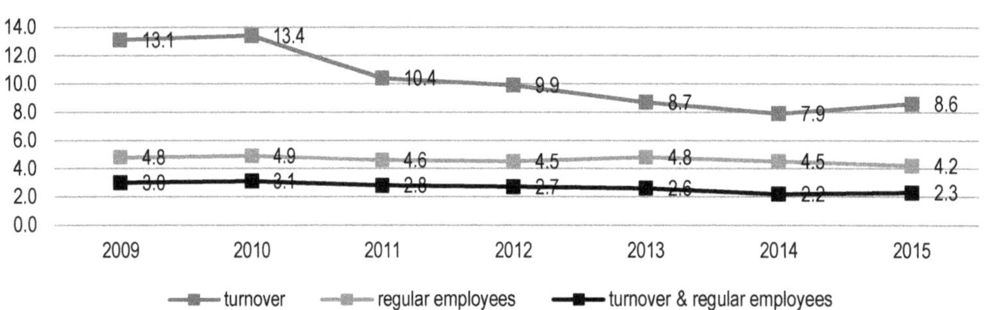

Note: High-growth enterprises are defined in Korea as enterprises which surpass 20% average in terms of sales or full-time employees. This differs slightly from the OECD definition, which defines high-growth enterprises as enterprises with average annualised growth in employees (or turnover) greater than 20% over a three-year period, and with ten or more employees at the beginning of the observation period. Gazelles are a subset of high-growth enterprises, i.e. those which have been employers only for a period of up to five years. The rates are calculated on the total number of employer enterprises with at least 10 employees at the beginning of the observation period.
Source: Statistics Korea.

Gazelle companies are a specific subset of high-growth enterprises; i.e. those aged less than 5 years at the beginning of the observation period. There are relatively small numbers of gazelles in Seoul: 299 measured by turnover and employees and 854 measured by turnover only in 2015. This stands in contrast to the very high rate of graduates in science, technology and innovation (STI) in Korea and can point to structural and perceptual barriers to innovative entrepreneurship and SME development.

3.2. SME and entrepreneurship development challenges require action

3.2.1. Low domestic demand and declining exports call for a strengthened role of SMEs and entrepreneurship

Seoul faces a number of macroeconomic and structural challenges, which affect SMEs and entrepreneurship, including increased competition from emerging economies, an ageing population, and low domestic demand coupled with high household debt (Chapter 1). Although growth in Korea is still higher than in the OECD, it has slowed significantly and steadily since the 1997 Asian financial crises. The five-year GDP average growth rate was 7.9% between 1991 and 1995, and then sustained a significant drop over the next two decades, reaching 2.8% between 2011 and 2015 (Figure 3.4, Panel A). The slowdown in GDP growth is closely linked to very low growth in domestic demand, which was negative between 2010-2014 and has remained weak ever since (Whang et al., 2015). Growth in Korea has been driven largely by the export sector, whose share as a percentage of GDP rose steadily from the 1970s, experiencing drops in the late1980s the late 1990s, and dropping again in 2012.(Figure 3.4, Panel B).

Figure 3.4. Korea GDP growth is affected by declining share of exports

A. GDP growth in per cent

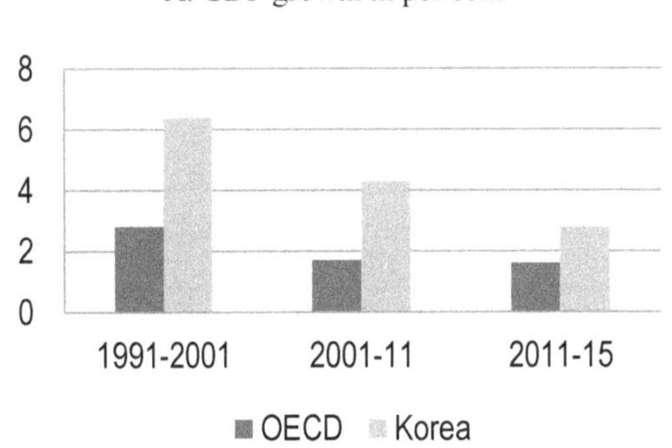

B. Exports as a percentage of GDP

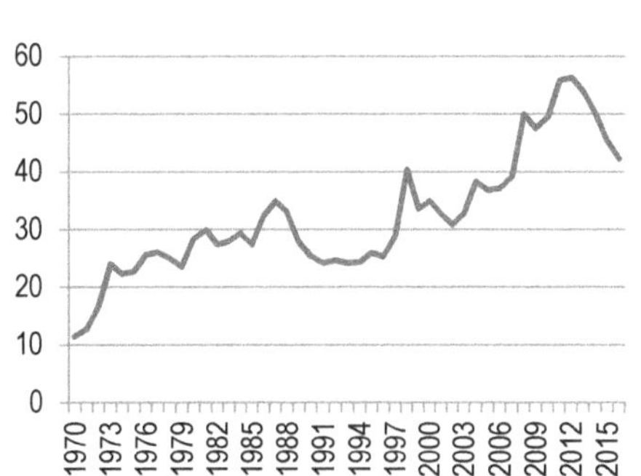

Source: OECD (2016b), and OECD Analytical Database.

One explanation for the slowdown of GDP lies in dampened spillover effects from the export sector. One important reason for this is the decrease of domestic value-added components in exports, which have declined from 76% in 1995 to below 60 % in 2011 (OECD, 2016a). This suggests that Korean firms are increasingly outsourcing to foreign supply chains instead of relying on local SMEs. This phenomenon has been observed across OECD countries as a result of the expansion of global value chains, implying a drop in the contribution of domestic value-added components to exports. This decrease is, however, also the consequence of some structural observations inherent to the Korean and Seoul economy, such as a large productivity gap between SMEs and large firms.

Productivity remains low in SMEs compared to large firms, affecting the distribution of economic growth

Efforts to foster business creation and increase the productivity of SMEs will be essential to the future development of Seoul. The growth of labour productivity in Korea has been the fastest in the OECD over the past 25 years at an annual average rate of nearly 5%. While this has helped raise per capita income, recent challenges have led to a slowdown and threaten further convergence to the highest income countries. Labour productivity per hour worked is still very low compared to OECD countries and can be mostly explained by low service sector productivity and low productivity in SMEs, which constitute about 87% of overall employment in the economy and also make up 90% of service-sector employment (OECD, 2016a). In the US, SMEs employ only 44% of workers in the service industry (Kim, 2015).

Labour productivity in SMEs is less than a third of that in large companies for all of Korea; the gap is widening, as labour productivity in SMEs fell from 53.8% of that in large companies in 1988 to 30.5% by 2014 (OECD, 2016a). This can partially be explained by the ability of large companies to scale-up investment in labour-saving technology and corresponding wage increases. Labour productivity of medium-sized companies (50-299 employees) in the wholesale and retail sector were only 62% of large firms and labour productivity of small firms (1-9 employees) was slightly above 20% of large firms (Figure 3.5). This stands in contrast to most OECD countries, where medium-sized companies outperform large firms' average productivity (OECD, 2017c).

Figure 3.5. Labour productivity gap between SMEs and large firms

Labour productivity in wholesale and retail trade[1] in 2012:
labour productivity for large firms (250+ employees) is set at 100[2]

A. Firms with 1-9 employees

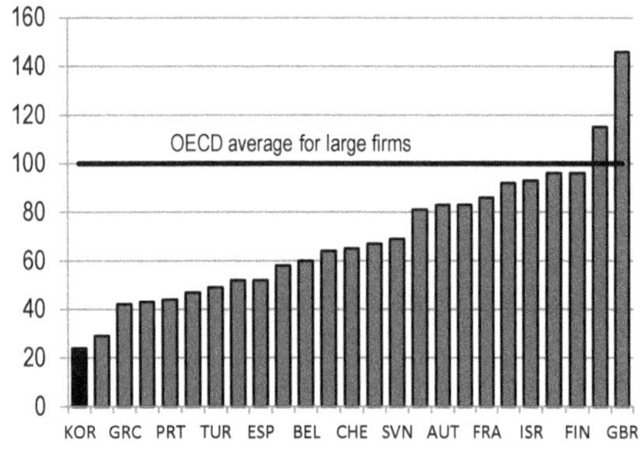

B. Firms with 49-250 employees

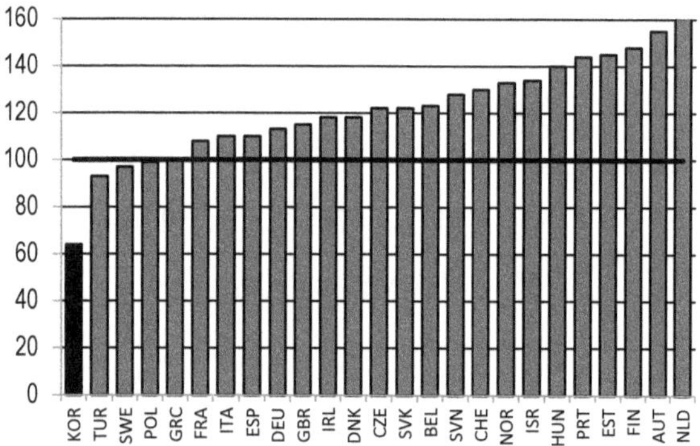

Note: 1) Includes the repair of motor vehicles and motorcycles; 2) For Korea, the size class "50-249" refers to "50-299" and the size class "250+" refers to "300+".
Source: OECD (2016a).

Low SME productivity and low levels of technology diffusion to small firms call for new policy measures to stimulate growth. The dominant role of large conglomerates (chaebols) poses challenges to SME and entrepreneurship development. Most SMEs rely on domestic consumption in their initial phase, which limits their growth possibilities. In many countries, one of the ways through which SMEs access wider international markets is through participation in the value chains of larger internationally-oriented enterprises.

While some SMEs in Seoul have been partnering with large corporations, the *chaebol*s are increasingly internationalising their supply chain, making it more difficult for small firms to access international markets and to profit from knowledge generation and technology diffusion through the supply chain. Limited market access also affects SME bargaining power and ability to compete.

A large gap persists between large firm and SME innovation

Favourable framework conditions and a dynamic business sector are crucial to an inclusive entrepreneurship ecosystem, which enables all groups of the population to participate in productive entrepreneurial activities. Innovation is key to increasing productivity in small firms and can take various forms, including the adoption of new products or the adoption of new methods for production, firm organisation or marketing. Innovation can also go beyond firm benefits and seek answers to social problems in local communities and places. Such innovations are defined by the OECD as social innovations as they aim at enhancing the welfare of individuals and communities through entrepreneurial solutions (OECD, 2017d). Cities and regions play an important role in driving social innovations through incorporating it in regional development agendas or through the development of social innovation centres (Box 3.2).

Most firms adopt mixed methods of innovation that include new marketing or organisational methods alongside product or process innovations, suggesting complementarities between different types of innovation. Although the share of innovative SMEs is still lower in Korean and Seoul than in other OECD countries, SMEs are active in many types of innovation in addition to R&D (Figure 3.6). A large gap remains, however, between the share of SMEs that innovate (30.2%) versus the share of large firm innovation (59.6%) in Korea overall. Although full comparability is difficult, as different surveys are used to measure, for example, innovation in firms in the European Union and Korea, this nevertheless confirms the efforts by Seoul Metropolitan Government to strengthen innovation, raise awareness and provide support for non-technological and social innovation in micro-enterprises.

Figure 3.6. SMEs innovation by type compared to large firm total innovation, 2012 - 2014

Percentage of all SMES and all large firms

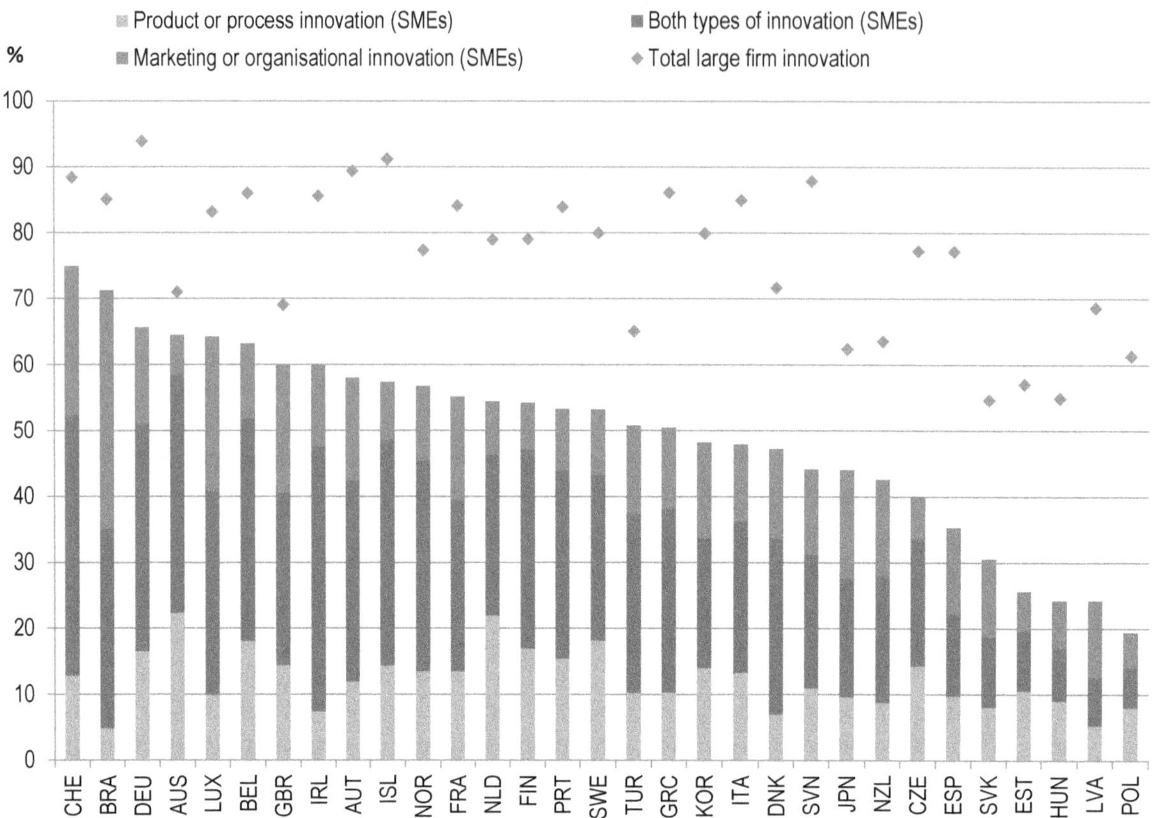

Note: International comparability may be limited due to differences in innovation survey methodologies and country-specific response patterns. European countries follow harmonised survey guidelines with the Community Innovation Survey. For Korea, data come from the Korean Innovation Survey. The survey is carried out separately for manufacturing and services, but both sets of data refer to 2013-15. Data do not include ongoing or abandoned innovative activities. The phrasing of the question on product innovation is slightly different from the guidelines given in the Oslo Manual. As a result the introduction of new services by manufacturing firms or of new goods by service firms might be under reported. Sectoral coverage is smaller than CIS for the industrial sector and includes ISIC Rev.4 Section C Manufacturing only. All services are covered except for Section (O) Public administration and defence; compulsory social security. Please see www.oecd.org/sti/inno-stats.htm for more details.
Source: OECD (2017e).

Although not all innovation is based on R&D, the propensity to introduce new products among firms performing R&D is usually higher. R&D is typically concentrated among the global players at the technology frontier, which is usually dominated by large firms. Although Korea has the highest share of GDP invested in R&D in the OECD and a large share of business R&D (Business enterprise Expenditure on Research and Development; BERD), the main source of R&D remain large manufacturing conglomerates. They account for more than two-thirds of R&D in Korea, while SMEs (excluding micro-firms with less than five workers) account for another 30%. R&D per large firm in 2010 was more than 100 times greater than in core SMEs, reflecting their lower technological and financial capabilities (OECD, 2016a). These obstacles call for local and national government to actively support innovation in SMEs.

A range of activities have been undertaken, including raising budgets for SME innovation support and the provision of R&D tax credits by the national government. Complementing and improving existing initiatives, local and regional governments have several instruments at their disposal to support innovative entrepreneurship among different groups of the population. This includes innovation grants and vouchers, but also measures of knowledge transfer, such as business incubators and accelerators and open innovation networks (see also Section 3.3).

Data from Seoul Metropolitan Statistics show that on average 78.3% of all products bought by public institutions in Seoul were produced by SMEs over the past decade (Table 3.4). This is a high figure which could be further leveraged by adding, for example, distinct innovation criteria to public procurement or products bought by SMEs.

Table 3.4. Public procurement of SME products by public institutions in Seoul, 2006-2016

Year	Total amount of public buying (KRW 1M)	Amount of buying SMEs' products (KRW 1M)	Ratio (%)
2006	1 577 515	1 547 739	98
2008	2 060 942	1 712 401	83
2010	3 861 153	2 516 210	65
2012	2 946 922	2 002 493	68
2014	3 139 555	2 316 155	74
2016	3 743 244	2 997 752	80

Source: Seoul Statistics.

Box 3.2. Social Impact Factory: A business support structure founded by the City of Utrecht, the Netherlands

The Social Impact Factory is a business support structure that was launched in 2014 as a joint initiative by the city of Utrecht and the firm Kirkman company. Based in Utrecht, the Social Impact Factory gained legal status in 2015 as a *stichting* (foundation) with a supervisory board. Its "founding partners" comprise a group of traditional businesses, social entrepreneurs and one community organisation, each contributing time and financial support, according to their capacity. Its objective is to inspire and connect partners to create an enabling environment ("ecosystem") for inclusive and social entrepreneurship. The Factory acts as a connector and conductor, federating the ecosystem by aligning its members' efforts and actions through its three different service pillars: social procurement, impact challenges and change-making:

- *Social procurement:* In January 2016, the Social Impact Factory launched the "Social Impact Market", an online business-to-business (B2B) marketplace for companies (including social enterprises) seeking opportunities to purchase social products or services.
- *Impact Challenge:* The Social Impact Factory has designed a model that connects different stakeholders to solve a specific societal challenge in an entrepreneurial way, thereby achieving social impact.
- *Change-making:* This pillar integrates the Factory's various efforts to accelerate fair, sustainable and inclusive business practices. The Factory organises events on inclusive and social entrepreneurship, including entrepreneurial training activities.

Since mid-2015, the Social Impact Factory has built a network of over 90 social entrepreneurs, 7 large traditional businesses and 15 municipalities across the Netherlands.

Source: OECD (2017d).

Entrepreneurial attitudes are lower in Korea and Seoul than in other countries despite higher trust in entrepreneurial skills

Positive entrepreneurial attitudes such as self-confidence, risk management, strategic thinking and team management are important levers of successful entrepreneurship. Data from the adult population survey from the Global Entrepreneurship Monitoring (GEM) research consortium show that entrepreneurial attitudes in the Korean population (aged 18-64), which can be considered as representative for Seoul, are generally lower than the average of the 27 participating OECD countries. Around 45% of the population considered entrepreneurship in 2016 as a desirable career option compared to 53% in the OECD. The perceived social status of entrepreneurship was nevertheless nearly as high as in the OECD, with 60% to 62% in the OECD. A higher than OECD average number of Koreans believed to have the skills to start a business and entrepreneurial intentions relative to the OECD average, with 27% to 18%. Only 32 % indicated that fear of failure would prevent them from establishing a business. Despite these positive indications, only 35% of the Korean people saw however an opportunity to start a business in the place where they lived. This could be an indication of structural barriers to entrepreneurship in a generally entrepreneurship-friendly environment (Figure 3.7).

Early stage entrepreneurial activity, as measured by the percentage of the 18-64 population who are either a nascent entrepreneur or owner-manager of a business with fewer than 42 months is low in Korea compared to the OECD average. Korea's Total Early-Stage Entrepreneurial Activity (TEA) rate was 6.7% in 2016 compared to an OECD average of 12.2%. Out of this rate, 2.7% have been driven by perceived market opportunities or the desire to improve one own's conditions in terms of income or independence. This also implies a relatively large share of necessity-driven entrepreneurship and confirms the need to improve local conditions for under-represented and disadvantaged groups in entrepreneurship and business ownership to fully reap the benefits of entrepreneurship.

Figure 3.7. Entrepreneurial attitudes in the Korean adult population, 2016

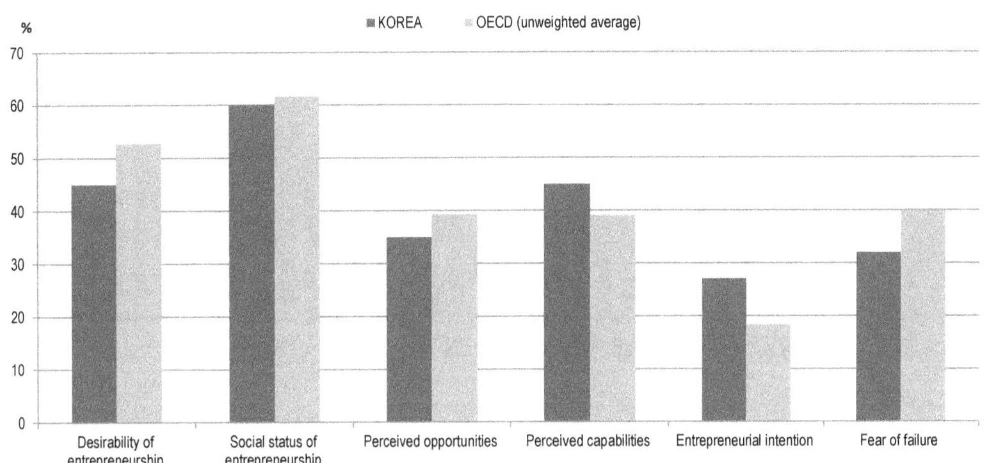

Note: Percentage values are out of the total adult population (18-64), except for "fear of failure" which is out of those who "perceive a market opportunity". This is the exact definition for each indicator: i) Desirability of entrepreneurship: Percentage of 18-64 population who agree with the statement that in their country, most people consider starting a business as a desirable career choice; ii) Social status of entrepreneurship: Percentage of 18-64 population who agree with the statement that in their country, successful entrepreneurs receive high status; iii) Perceived opportunities: Percentage of 18-64 who see good opportunities to start a firm in the area where they live; iv) Perceived capabilities: Percentage of 18-64 population who believe to have the required skills and knowledge to start a business v) Entrepreneurial intention: Percentage of 18-64 population (individuals involved in any stage of entrepreneurial activity excluded) who intend to start a business within three years; vi) Fear of failure: Percentage of 18-64 population with positive perceived opportunities who indicate that fear of failure would prevent them from setting up a business. Data exclude New Zealand and Iceland.
Source: OECD based on data supplied by the Global Entrepreneurship Monitor (GEM) research consortium.

Regulatory simplification has the potential to drive entrepreneurial dynamics in Seoul

The policy environment plays an important role in encouraging new business creation and promoting competition in the economy. Business creation is facilitated through less red tape and low financial and regulatory barriers. The OECD Product Market Regulation Index measures to which degree policies promote or inhibit competition and innovative entrepreneurship by creating barriers to business entry or growth. The Index is composed of three components, the level of state control, barriers to entrepreneurship, and barriers to trade and investment. Korea's overall index score was the fourth most stringent in the OECD in 2013.

Barriers to entrepreneurship were seventh highest in Korea compared to OECD countries in 2013 (Figure 3.8). This implies relatively high entry barriers to new business creation, which is needed to boost productivity growth (Koske et al., 2015). A study on regulation and industrial performance across Korean sectors found that higher entry regulations reduced both entries and exits, thus limiting entrepreneurial dynamism (Ahn, 2015). The OECD Product Market Regulation (PMR) Index further shows that entry barriers in Korea are higher in services than manufacturing, which is largely dominated by SMEs, thus putting a higher regulatory burden on small firms.

Figure 3.8. Barriers to entrepreneurship across the OECD, 2013

Scale from 0 to 6 from least to most restrictive

■ Administrative burdens on startups ■ Complexity of regulatory procedures ■ Regulatory protection of incumbents ◇ Barriers tp emtrepreneurship, 2003

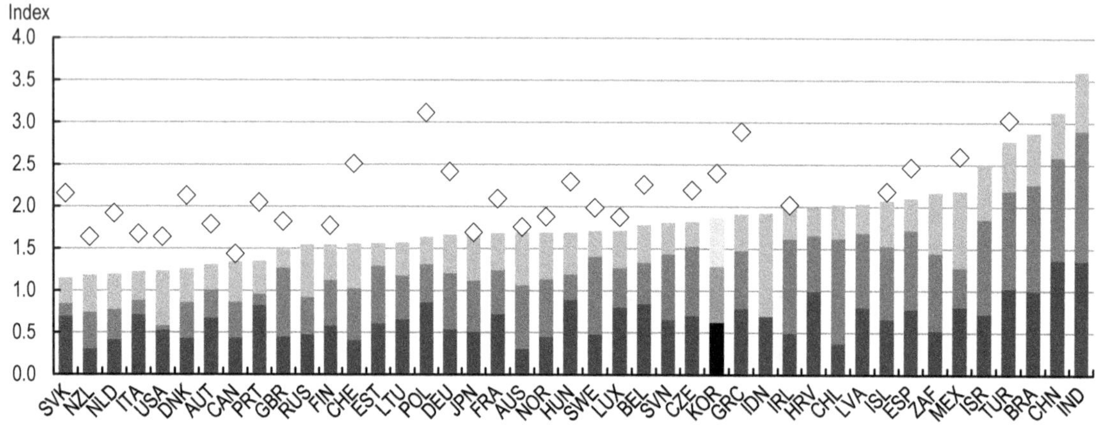

Source: OECD (2015c), Product Market Regulation (database), www.oecd.org/economy/pmr.

The regulatory burden on new business creation is also captured through the World Bank Doing Business Survey which measures business regulations across several dimensions for small and medium sized firms in 150 countries worldwide (Figure 3.9). The data for Korea have been exclusively gathered from Seoul, the survey is thus representative for both the country and the capital. Overall, Korea ranks fourth out of 190 countries on the ease of starting a business, suggesting that lengthy and costly business regulations do not affect entrepreneurship in Seoul. Korea and Seoul rank lower on providing access to credit, registering property and trading across borders, suggesting that barriers to SME development remain despite overall good business start-up conditions.

Figure 3.9. Ease of creating a small business in Korea, 2016

The ease of doing business ranking ranges from 1-190, with 1 being best and 190 worst.

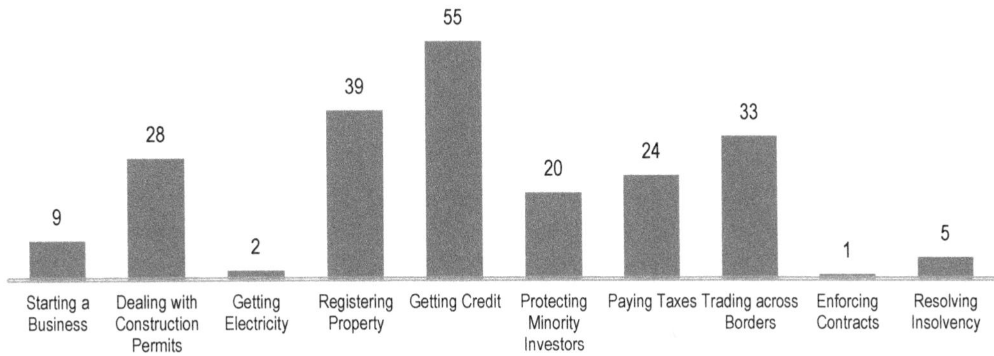

Source: World Bank (2016), Doing Business Korea.

Labour market dualism presents a challenge for Seoul and calls for better integration of youth and women into entrepreneurship activities

Rigid labour markets, combined with rising youth inactivity rates and weak labour participation among women, highlight the need for a social equity agenda that creates a level playing field for self-employment and business creation among all parts of Seoul's population. Labour market efforts are needed in order to promote greater flexibility and give entrepreneurship and small firms a stronger role in driving inclusive growth.

Wage is one component that bridges gaps within the labour market and a key policy target for inclusive growth. Korea and Seoul are characterised by wide wage dispersion and a high share of low-wage workers. In 2013, nearly a quarter of full-time workers earned less than two thirds of the medium wage, which is the second highest share in the OECD after the US (OECD, 2016a).

One of the reasons for high income and wage inequality is the particularly high labour market dualism in Korea (Box 3.4), resulting in a high share of non-regular workers. This group of workers includes fixed-term, part-time and dispatched workers and has accounted for more than half of all employees in Seoul (Table 3.5) and a third of all employees in Korea overall during the past decade

Table 3.5. Non-regular workers account for half of workforce in Seoul

Employed persons by status of employee in Seoul, 2006 - 2017

	Wage workers	Non-regular workers	
	Thousand	Thousand	%
2006	2051	1 486	72.5
2008	2250	1 391	61.8
2010	2484	1 303	52.4
2012	2579	1 311	50.8
2014	2701	1289	47.7
2017	2716	1378	50.7

Source: OECD (2016a); Statistics Korea, Economically Active Population Survey.

Non-regular workers face a range of challenging employment conditions compared to regular workers:

- ***Wage differences***: in 2016 the average monthly wage of non-regular workers in Seoul was 55.1% of that of regular workers; the average hourly wage of non-regular workers was 66.3% of that of regular workers.
- ***Weaker social security***: non-regular workers have less access to social safety nets and face greater threats of poverty. In 2011, the relative poverty rate was 16% in a household headed by a non-regular worker (OECD, 2016a).
- ***Limited employment stability and advancement***: A study by Lee & Shin (2017) found that non-regular employment is not a stepping stone to regular employment, but a 'dead-end trap,' and called for policy action.
- ***Reduced skills and training opportunities***: Non-regular workers have less access to training provided by firms since the time delimited nature of contracts reduces incentives for firms to invest in them, thus further reducing their skills accumulation and earning power (Hara, 2014).

In Korea, vulnerable populations are more likely to be in non-regular positions. For example, 35% of youth under the age of 30 have non-regular positions compared to 27% of those between the age of 30-59; the elderly are also in precarious employment situations, with 67% of those 60 years and older holding non-regular positions. Women also represent a larger share of non-regular workers: 40% compared to men at 27%. Education continues to play a role in employment opportunities, as those without high school degrees or higher also tend to be over represented in non-regular employment (Table 3.6).

Table 3.6. Non-regular employment is most prevalent among small firms, women, youth and older workers and the less educated

Percentage share of non-regular employment by category (August 2015)

Size of establishment	**Below 5**	**5 to 299**	**Above 30**
	47.5	31.7	14.0
Age	**Under 30**	**30 to 59**	**Above 60**
	35.0	26.8	67.4
Gender	**Male**	**Female**	
	26.5	40.2	
Education	**Middle school or less**	**High school**	**Tertiary**
	59.9	37.1	21.4
Sector	**Manufacturing**	**Wholesale and retail**	**Construction**
	13.7	28.9	52.3

Source: OECD 2016a; Statistics Korea, Economically Active Population Survey.

Non-regular workers are also largely present in micro and small businesses, which confirm the strong labour market duality between large and small firms. Businesses with fewer than 5 employees had a share of 47.5% non-regular employers as opposed to 14% in large businesses with 300+ employees. As non-regular workers also have wages within 60-70% of regular workers, a large wage gap exists according to employment type and firm size, leaving micro enterprises with low wage non-regular workers (Figure 3.10)

Figure 3.10. Average hourly wage for regular and non-regular workers by firm size in Korea, 2016

Total hourly wages (KRW)

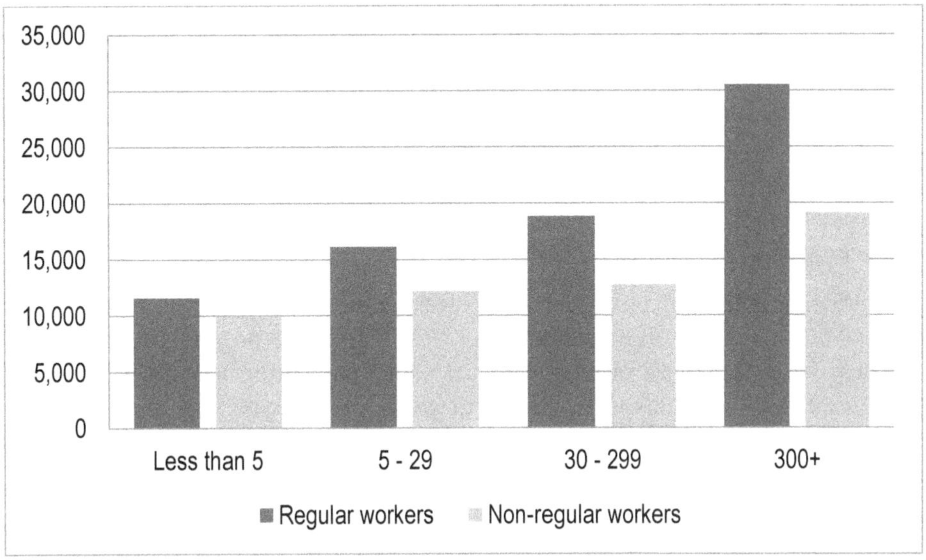

Source: Ministry of Employment and Labor of Korea (2017).

As labour market dualism in Korea and Seoul is highly stratified along the lines of education, skills, and gender, policies are needed that break down the strong divide between regular and non-regular employment and secure high-quality employment and self-employment opportunities for disadvantaged and under-represented parts of the population.

Expanding employment opportunities for women, youth, and seniors is key to combatting demographic trends and strengthening inclusive entrepreneurship and SME development in Seoul. The employment rate of women in Korea was the ninth lowest in the OECD in 2017 and 19.3 percentage points below that of men (OECD, 2016b). A high share of women exit the workforce following marriage and childbirth and return to the labour market at a later age, facing lower career and earning opportunities. Self-employment and business creation can be an alternative to the labour market if women have equal opportunity to start and run businesses. This includes improving maternity and parental leave systems and availability of high-quality childcare, and to facilitate re-enter into the workforce after long absences (Box 3.3).

Box 3.3. Women in the Labour Market, Croatia

How to support unemployed women in business creation

The project "Women in the Labour Market" is run by the Croatian Employment Service (CES) and aims to increase the employability of disadvantaged women and support their entry into the labour market. The project targets unemployed women over the age of 40, women who had been unemployed for at least 12 months, and those note active in the workforce. The main rationale for launching this initiative was to reduce the labour market disadvantages against Croatian women who had difficulties entering the labour market after a period of inactivity.

The grant scheme launched in August 2009 offering grants in the amount of EUR 90 000 to EUR 140 000. Eligible organisations proposed 12-month projects of for featuring a range of activities, including provision of assistance and information on labour market opportunities. Several projects were offered grants in different regions of the country. The projects ranged from:

- ***Business development training:*** training programmes offered participants basic entrepreneurship skills, business planning, business management, marketing, accounting, financial planning, computer skills, and communications know-how.
- ***Communications resources***: development of publications, manuals and websites.
- ***Networking***: organisation of business-to-business meetings connecting participating women and potential employers.

The programme enabled numerous institutions at the national, regional (i.e. county) and local levels to develop know-how and supports for various important vulnerable groups. The 3 projects selected supported unemployed women in business creation and 105 women into self-employment or paid employment in the first two years.

Source: OECD (2017f).

Although youth unemployment has fallen significantly since 2004 in Korea, 18% of all youth were neither in employment, education or training (NEET) in 2014 (Chapter 1). Korea is also one of the few countries where the rate of NEETs with tertiary education is higher than the overall 15-29 age group. Skills mismatch is especially acute within the educated youth population, youth also fall victim to the high labour market dualism as the rising number of graduates outnumber newly created high-quality jobs (Kim, 2015). Lower wages and weaker job security make SMEs less attractive and entrepreneurship is not always perceived as a desirable career choice (Kim, 2015). Policy-makers at local and national level have a role here to play in reducing the dualism between regular and non-regular workers and render boosting entrepreneurship and business creation (Box 3.4).

Box 3.4. Chaebols and SMEs in Korea

Korea's labour market is characterised by a duality between primary and secondary markets. The primary market consists of large business groups or *chaebols*. These are a collection of legally independent firms operating in multiple industries subject to *de facto* centralised control by the same person. They operate under tight regulation, such as on their intra-group shareholding, trading and debt guarantees that are aimed at limiting their economic power. They attract high-skilled workers by offering regular employment with generous benefits and career opportunities.

The secondary market is populated by SMEs, mostly labour-intense service providers working as subcontractors to *chaebols*. They rely much less on innovation and compete on costs rather than with innovative products. *Chaebols* have a holdout power over them, curbing their profitability. Bankruptcy and reorganisation rates are also high among SMEs. SMEs are regulated much more loosely than *chaebols* and are effectively exempted from labour standards. Given the larger share of non-regular workers in SMEs, many are not covered by social insurance. In addition, as many are fixed-term workers, firms provide less training for non-regular workers, thereby limiting their prospects for advancement.

Source: OECD (2016a); Hlasny (2017).

3.3. The *Economic Democratisation Agenda*: An important policy lever for entrepreneurship and SME development in Seoul

The *Economic Democratisation Agenda* (EDA), introduced by SMG in 2016, is an important policy response to many challenges facing small business owners, as well as other vulnerable workers and economic sectors. The EDA aims to reduce economic inequality and provide equal opportunity for all citizens to engage in sustainable economic activities. The agenda identifies 23 measures under three categories of 'partnership', 'fairness' and 'labour', which aim to eradicate unfair competition and support underprivileged and disadvantaged groups (Table 3.7). Some of these measures are targeted at groups of individuals, and others at supporting SMEs and entrepreneurship.

Table 3.7. Seoul's Economic Democratisation Agenda

23 measures introduced by Seoul Metropolitan Government

Overarching objective	Target of policy intervention	Specific measures
Partnership	**Support for SMEs**	Support for neighbourhood and small enterprises to strengthen capability to grow businesses
		Protection and invigoration of SMEs
		Enhancement of cooperation between large conglomerates and neighbourhood businesses
		Reinforcement of technological protection support for start-ups and SMEs
		Implementation of an outcome-sharing model between public institutions under SMG
	Support for financially vulnerable	Support for the financially underprivileged
		Support for young people to engage in sound financial activities
		Provision of a second chance to small business owners with financial difficulties
		Financial guarantees at a reasonable interest rate for small business owners
Fairness	**Unfair business transactions**	Prevention of unfair franchise-related transaction practices
		Elimination of unfair subcontracting practices in the construction industry
		Provision of relief on damages caused by unfair practices of the art industry
	Interactions between producers and consumers	Protection of consumers' rights and benefits
		Restraint of illegal activities threatening people's livelihood
	Building leases	Protection of tenants' rights to ensure stable businesses
		Implementation and promotion of fair commercial lease system
		Protection of tenants and their businesses from relocation caused by urban regeneration projects
Labour market	**Levelling the playing field in the labour market**	Social insurance support for small business owners
		Introduction of worker-director system for government-funded institutions
		Facilitation of the early implementation of the living wage system
		Conversion of non-regular workers to permanent work positions in the public sector
		Prevention of overdue wages of part-time workers and provision of relief
		Imposing obligations to pay prevailing wages to construction workers

Source: Seoul Metropolitan Government (2017), Background Questionnaire provided to OECD.

3.3.1. Important challenges faced by SMEs and entrepreneurs are highlighted by the Economic Democratisation Agenda

The EDA includes important features aimed to strengthen inclusive entrepreneurship and SME development, and highlights a number of challenges faced by large parts of the population engaged in SME and entrepreneurship activities. These include low levels of productivity, difficulties in accessing finance, unfair franchise practices and commercial leases, and specific labour market challenges faced by workers.

Supporting managerial skills in small businesses increases SME innovation and productivity

The EDA includes a range of important measures to support SME productivity and sustainability. Strengthening the capability of small firm owner-managers to sustain their businesses is vital for SMEs and entrepreneurs to be able to compete on an equal-playing field. Several studies have shown that strengthening managerial and organisational capital in small and neighbourhood businesses has implications for firm survival and growth (Bruhn et al., 2010; Bloom and van Reenen, 2007). Such managerial skills include the capacity of business owners to improve the marginal productivity of their firm's inputs, such as labour or physical capital, but also to deal with the small business capital structure and business plan. These skills require either training or experience from other well-run firms or might be acquired through outside consulting inputs, which public policy can provide, particularly for micro-enterprises. Positive effects of consulting services on managerial knowledge have been shown in Bruhn et al. (2010), who conducted a randomised control trial on managerial consulting in Mexico and found that monthly firm sales and profits were higher in the treatment group who had received the consulting (78% and 110%, respectively). Such small firm business support is a targeted policy that is very often delivered at the local level. In the case of Seoul, it would be important to ensure that support reaches out the firms in need and meets their productivity challenges.

Open innovation networks foster collaboration between large and small firms

The EDA also recognises the importance of an open innovation system, which seeks to encourage collaboration between large and small companies and with academia (Enkel, Gassmann, and Chesbrough, 2009). Larger businesses can contribute to and engage with SMEs to develop partnerships and networks through the principles of co-creation and co-development. Both small and large firms benefit from open innovation by increasing their reach for new ideas and customers, reducing costs for innovation when shared and scaling up the speed of innovation (Zahra and Nambisan, 2012, Box 3.5). There may also be wider social benefits from open innovation, for example through the introduction of new products and services from improved innovation. Policy has a key role in supporting open innovation in different ways (Roper, 2016) and the EDA rightly envisages some of them. A key role for local policy-makers lies in raising awareness of the benefits of open innovation, for example through events or network-based activities, which help firms connect with each other. The Seoul Metropolitan Government can act as an advocate here to build networks and promote open innovation and brokering between large and small firms.

Box 3.5. Interface: The knowledge connection supporting open innovation in Scotland

Interface is a service created in 2005 which aims to link small businesses and industry with academia. Interface works with 24 partner research and higher education institutes in Scotland. Its main objectives are to encourage increased open innovation and the commercialisation of research, and also to promote Scottish universities and their collaboration with businesses. Although no restrictions on participation by size exist, most companies supported in practice are SMEs.

Interface mainly provides a match-making support scheme, with staff in the organisation providing information on capability and capacity in the Universities in response to business enquiries. Enquiries when they are received from firms are filtered and directed to individual research and commercialisation offices in each university. Interface identifies the university or research institute that matches the needs of a company asking for support, and checks their capability to support the company and the interest raised. Typically, two weeks are given to respond and therefore to organise match-making if the assessment is positive. Contacts are monitored until they either result in an agreed partnership or are closed. Around 40 % of initial enquiries result in a collaborative project or agreement.

Source: www.interface-online.org.uk.

Financial support to entrepreneurs and SMEs can help correct market failures and help small businesses thrive

Access to finance is often identified as one of the greatest barriers to start and grow a business, and is recognised as such in the EDA. This challenge is magnified for disadvantaged and under-represented groups, reflecting their lack of collateral assets and financial resources (OECD, 2015a). The goal of public policy should be that everyone can access business financing tools irrespective of age and gender. Grants are the most common approach used by OECD countries to support inclusive entrepreneurship. Many small business owners also apply for bank loans, however not always with success as many are rejected due to a lack of collateral. Public policy can intervene in different ways, such as by targeting loans to people who would otherwise find it difficult to obtain them but who have a viable business plan. Alternatively, policy makers can offer a guarantee on private sector loans. These credit guarantee schemes are a commitment by the state to secure the loan if the borrower fails to repay. When it comes to risk-financing beyond the start-up phase, investments are more suitable than loans to finance high-risk firms.

While the EDA highlights the need to support small businesses financially, SMG needs to carefully design programmes to avoid deadweight costs, displacement effects and gain support for non-viable companies (Box 3.6). As pointed out by Chang (2016), a productive SME support policy should correct market failures and support SME contribution to job creation and output growth. The emphasis of Korea's current national policy lies too much on supporting firm survival instead of productivity, and current programs have lowered the productivity of recipient firms and increased the survival probability of incompetent ones. Setting up productivity-enhancing financial support measures and introducing an adequate monitoring system which allows for restructuring where needed is important for SMG to strengthen inclusive entrepreneurship and SME development.

Box 3.6. What SME and entrepreneurship policy should avoid

High deadweight costs

The extent to which participants would have set up a new business without the subsidy. Since behaviour of these "deadweight participants" is unaffected by the scheme, their participation does not contribute to the economic value generated, but involves a public outlay. The social cost of this outlay is the sum of the distortionary cost or excess burden of the tax that finances it.

Displacement effects

The extent to which subsidised businesses take business from and displace employment in unsubsidised business. Policies should not support displacements.

Support for non-viable companies

Non-viable companies (often referred to as "zombie companies") are those with negative operating profits over three years. Keeping these companies alive through poorly designed financial support instruments lowers the growth potential of the economy by preventing the allocation of financial resources to productive companies and preventing the exit of unproductive firms.

Inclusive entrepreneurship requires strengthening self-employment

Inclusive entrepreneurship policies have an important role in addressing the quality of the businesses started by people from under-represented and disadvantaged social groups (OECD, 2017g). This includes policies and programmes that assist under-represented and disadvantaged groups in the labour market (i.e. women, youth, seniors, the unemployed, immigrants and people with disabilities) in starting and growing businesses. The objective is to move more people into work via self-employment to allow people to participate economically and socially, and to generate income. It is also important that people acquire skills and experience by participating in entrepreneurship programmes and starting businesses, which then increases their overall employability.

Many of the small businesses in Seoul have low turnover and low levels of growth. Improving the quality of these businesses will have a direct impact on an entrepreneur's life by increasing their income, standard of living, and well-being. This will also result in economic benefits as higher quality businesses are less likely to exit and more likely to contribute more to aggregate economic performance. A multi-pronged approach should be used to combat labour market dualism, and SMG and the EDA play a major role in designing and implementing policies that improve the employment and wage status of employees in small businesses. Measures such as social insurance support and the introduction of a living-wage system are vital in this regard.

3.3.2. A range of important public policy measures have been taken to support implementation of the EDA

SMG has initiated many initiatives to mitigate the negative impacts on disadvantaged and underprivileged segments of both the SME sector and individuals. The Small Business Development Centre provides **support and business development services** (BDS) to entrepreneurs and SMEs at all stages. The SMG Small Business Division further provides BDS to SMEs and entrepreneurs in the form of training and access to loan subsidies and consultants. As of July 2017, it has trained 12 847 people as potential entrepreneurs, provided mentoring and advise to 5 328 start-ups, supported 1 376 individuals to grow their business, and helped launch 15 new cooperatives.

The SBDC's **second chance programme** is an excellent initiative to address the stigma of failure. It provides support to businesses with a tax default status who would like a second chance, by lifting the delinquent borrower status and halting the seizure of deposits or vehicles. This has benefitted 50 727 individuals to date. The programme provides loan guarantees to business owners with poor credit ratings so they can profit from mid-interest rate loans in the range of 5% to 8% (this has been supported in 409 cases).

Several policy measures have also been undertaken to **strengthen SME innovation.** Most of these measures are targeted at protecting SMEs and need to be complemented with incentives to innovate and compete on the market. The Seoul Technology Protection Group is an important instrument for legal and financial support for litigation on breaches of intellectual property rights of SMEs.

Important **labour market measures** have been introduced by SMG, among them social insurance support to small business owners in the form of long-term, low-interest guarantees and loans. SMG has further supported the implementation of a living-wage system to private sector employees and has started the transition to convert non-regular workers into permanent work in the public sector, while lobbying for private sector to follow the example.

In order to make EDA a successful policy instrument to boost inclusive entrepreneurship, **co-ordination among all stakeholders** in charge of implementation is vital. This ideally requires the establishment of an action plan and a co-ordinating secretariat that monitors and evaluates outcomes against set targets on a regular basis. Work in policy silos and a lack of co-ordination would endanger the success and implementation of EDA.

3.3.3. The EDA helps address challenges facing youth, women and the elderly in the labour market.

Youth, women, and the elderly face higher barriers to entrepreneurship in a number of areas in Seoul, such as increased difficulties in accessing finance through a lack of collateral, weaker entrepreneurship skills and competences, more negative attitudes to failure, and smaller business networks relative to other entrepreneurs. These are constraints to both social inclusion and economic growth through a more broad-based and inclusive entrepreneurship.

The EDA recognises the need to address barriers that youth face in sustainable business creation and development and addresses them by proposing a range of support measures. These include training, advice on technology development and network building. The importance of supporting women in the labour market is also recognised. Supporting women in creating businesses in higher value-added sectors and supporting entrepreneurial training for youth and women – particularly in Science, Technology, Engineering, and Mathematics (STEM) fields –will create more sustainable businesses that pay higher wages and promote well-being in the long-run. Measures like the Job Cafés offering employment consultation to youth are important initiatives in this regard. They need to be complemented with further activities to raise the profile of entrepreneurship and solidify support for viable business ideas (Box 3.7). Given the large rate of tertiary university graduates struggling to find employment, more entrepreneurship education at universities and business incubators and accelerators supporting good ideas would also raise the profile of entrepreneurship.

Box 3.7. DreamStart, Belgium

Supporting unemployed youth in business creation

Launched in 2013, DreamStart is an integrated start-up scheme that supports unemployed youth (under 30 years old) in business creation in the Brussels region. It facilitates the acquisition of entrepreneurship skills through formal pre-start-up training as well as informal methods such as coaching and mentoring. Volunteers, experienced business professionals from public and private sector organisations, play a key role in delivering these services. Access to finance is facilitated through microfinance institutions who participate in the programme.

The primary intake mechanism for DreamStart is individual interviews that project managers have with potential clients. Three key criteria are used by project managers to select participants:

- their attitude towards becoming self-employed and their desire to start a business;
- the viability of the business idea and the anticipated results of the proposed product or service;
- the match between the business idea and the participant's professional and technical expertise and experience in that area.

Support officially ends once participants have developed their business plan and received feedback from an external evaluation panel. However, it is quite common for participants to form informal support groups in which they assist and advise each other.

Approximately 60% of youth who finish the scheme and present their plan to the panel start a business within a year. Monitoring shows that one-third of participants who complete the cycle work full-time in this activity and two-thirds work part-time and combine self-employment with paid employment. This allows them to finance their start-up with their earnings.

Source: OECD (2017f).

3.3.4. At national level, the incoming administration has already shown strong policy support for SMEs and entrepreneurship.

The government has elevated the Small and Medium Business Administration (SMBA) to a cabinet ministry, henceforth the Ministry of SMEs and Start-ups. Other priorities include providing stronger government support for SMEs and start-ups, preventing discrimination against temporary and contract workers, and increasing welfare for working parents, including childcare. The government has also approved legislation to increase the hourly minimum wage by 16.4% in 2018. Although the government plans to inject KRW 3 trillion to support SMEs in dealing with the financial impact of the minimum wage increase, such a measure could still negatively impact the competitiveness of many SMEs if they do not increase productivity.

Important changes have taken place at national level to support SME development, such as an upgrade of the innovation system to support technology transfer between small businesses, large firms and university collaboration. The government is further improving framework conditions to accelerate the implementation of innovation and strengthen inclusive labour markets. New start-up promotion has advanced at national level and funding support for SMEs in the creative economy has expanded since late 2015 (OECD, 2016a).

Seoul's efforts to level the playing field for SMEs and existing and potential entrepreneurs from disadvantaged groups would benefit from further structural reforms at national level. This could include addressing the structural challenges facing specific groups in the workforce (youth, women; non-regular workers), as well as creating a more level playing field for SMEs vis a vis the *chaebols*. The new national administration has demonstrated support for this agenda.

3.4. Moving forward: Strengthening support for SMEs and entrepreneurs for inclusive growth

To further strengthen the impact of the EDA, SMG could envisage some complementary strategies that aim to boost entrepreneurship among specific populations (such as women and youth); strengthen collaboration and networking for SMEs (with other SMEs, large firms, academia, etc.); and improve coordination at local and national levels to support SMEs and entrepreneurship and, more broadly, create a more inclusive labour market. Proposed recommendations for SMG are grouped into the following four categories: governance, entrepreneurial ecosystem, *skills* and *networks.*

3.4.1. Governance: Align the EDA with the city's overall strategic vision for economic development and inclusive growth and strengthen monitoring and evaluation efforts

Currently, there is limited co-ordination and collaboration across administrative departments in Seoul, although many of them are working on related policy challenges. Even within teams working on similar topics, there is not always strong coordination or shared objectives. These silos are individually undertaking important initiatives, but run the risk of duplication.

The EDA should be strengthened through **improved coordination within and across administrative departments**. While not easy, this process would cut across SMG departments and require strong coordination and collaboration among the different teams charged with designing and implementing individual initiatives. The EDA could have greater impact by ensuring clear alignment with the city's overall strategic vision for economic development and inclusive growth. This requires a clear understanding of how SMG can best align its policies with national policy; identify where it can build on these, and bridge gaps in existing policy efforts at local level to achieve its inclusive growth objectives. In concrete terms, the EDA should clearly complement and link to policy efforts in other relevant areas (e.g. efforts to expand childcare support for parents, efforts to reduce unemployment).

Finally, SMG could also **strengthen monitoring and evaluation** in order to measure the efficiency and impact of different policy measures of the EDA. A sound monitoring and evaluation system would include a developed logic of change, setting out expected results of the interventions. Intervention impacts should then be measured through key performance indicators (KPIs), which would demonstrate policy effectiveness and the efficiency of the implementation approach (Table 3.8). The evaluation techniques should be guided by the OECD Framework for the Evaluation of SME and Entrepreneurship Policies and Programmes (OECD, 2007).

Table 3.8. Criteria to evaluate inclusive entrepreneurship programmes and policies

Measure	Definition	Sample questions
Relevance	The extent to which the activity is suited to the priorities and policies of the target group, recipient and government (objectives vs. needs).	Is finance still a barrier to female entrepreneurship? Do changes in regulations related to benefits for the disabled make it impossible to start up a business?
Effectiveness	The extent to which the intervention's objectives were achieved, or are expected to be achieved, taking into account their relative importance (outcomes vs. objectives).	Was the target number of youth enterprises reached? Did they survive for two years?
Efficiency	Outputs in relation to inputs. This is an economic term signifying that the intervention uses the least costly resources in achieving desired results (inputs vs. outputs).	What was the cost per person advised? What was the cost per person per job created? What percentage of clients was from the target group? Were there more efficient was of implementing the action?
Impact	The positive and negative changes produced by a policy intervention, directly or indirectly, intended or unintended (objectives vs. outcomes).	Is there now a higher rate of business ownership and self-employment in the target group? Is there now a higher employment rate for the target group? Has social inclusion increased?
Sustainability	Whether the benefits of the activity are likely to continue after funding has been withdrawn.	Will the microcredit scheme established for senior entrepreneurs be self-financing? Is the advice centre capable of retaining the skills it has developed? Is there a need for further public support?

Source: Adapted from OECD (2007).

3.4.2. Entrepreneurial ecosystem: Creating supporting conditions in the business environment

Access to finance, skills, technology and knowledge are essential for innovative SME development and innovative entrepreneurship that will contribute the most to growing employment and income opportunities in the small business sector. The EDA identifies an important range of measures which will help develop more positive city-level business environment conditions.

In the context of inclusive growth, strengthening the city entrepreneurial ecosystem should stress inclusion of all population groups who can participate, including under-represented and disadvantaged groups. To this end, it is proposed to complement the EDA with i) policies that create an enabling business environment for SMEs and entrepreneurship and ii) targeted SME sector policies that aim to increase the competitiveness of SMEs and ultimately their contribution to growth and social inclusion (Box 3.8).

Box 3.8. An inclusive entrepreneurial ecosystem

An inclusive entrepreneurial ecosystem provides a holistic view of sustainable SME and entrepreneurship development. It involves a range of important stakeholders, including the government, the entrepreneurs themselves, large companies, media, and support organizations. The ecosystem begins with education, culture and human capital and the attitude of the local community to entrepreneurship which directly influences an individual's creative approach, attitude to risk and fear of failure. Additionally, the business environment plays a similar role in affecting obstacles likely to be encountered and the rewards to be achieved. Innovation and business development support, access to markets and appropriate affordable finance underpinned with sophisticated and inclusive business and investment networks complete the ecosystem (Figure 3.11).

Figure 3.11. Key elements of an inclusive entrepreneurship ecosystem

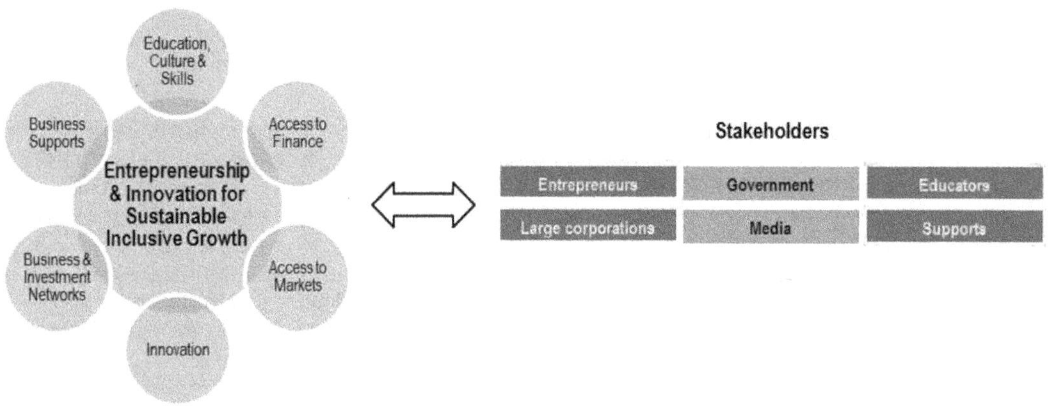

Acting in partnership with all key stakeholders, an ecosystem can be developed in Seoul that assists innovative small companies and start-ups from all segments of society. Lessons from the most effective policies and practices across OECD countries can provide the basis for choosing a set of interventions that work.

Source: Adapted from OECD (2015a).

3.4.3. Entrepreneurship skills: Provide entrepreneurship training and develop tailored skills support for disadvantaged and underrepresented groups

The **development of an entrepreneurial culture and mind-set** in society is a crucial element of creating sustainable businesses that contribute to social inclusion. Entrepreneurship and self-employment require a broad set of skills including risk management and opportunity recognition, as well as business management. Women and youth are more likely to lack entrepreneurship skills than men and evidence often points to different types of labour market experiences that offer fewer opportunities for them to obtain business management experience.

Public policy can help women and youth overcome this skills barrier through **entrepreneurship training, coaching and mentoring**. There is a growing trend for policy makers to focus such programmes on developing skills that would support business growth. Start-up training and consulting offered by the Small Business Development Centre could be further targeted towards these groups by either using specific training modules or by setting targets for the numbers of clients drawn from women and youth. The training should also be tailored to the needs and experiences of women and youth entrepreneurs, for example by using experienced female entrepreneurs as trainers or mentors.

SMG could also promote a positive attitude to entrepreneurship by introducing **role models and ambassadors**. Social attitudes and cultural views still tend to exert a negative influence on the local population's desire to start businesses, as well as on their self-confidence in managing a business. The policy goal should be to raise awareness about the potential of entrepreneurship and to increase all citizens' motivation for business creation and development. At the same time, women and youth entrepreneurship particularly needs encouragement to counter traditional career and gender stereotypes about activities of these groups in the labour market.

3.4.4. Networks: Integrate vulnerable groups into business networks and support collaborative projects between businesses to strengthen EDA effectiveness

SMG could consider a range of measures to increase networking by SMEs and entrepreneurs, including those from disadvantaged and under-represented groups. These networks can help small businesses and entrepreneurs gain access to markets, resources, knowledge and advice. This could be done in a variety of ways. For instance, SMG could introduce **policy support for collaborations among networks of SMEs for market access**. SMEs could be encouraged to work together for exporting or to develop partnerships with larger enterprises to enter into their value chains.

SMG could also develop **collaborative R&D projects**. Most business R&D spending happens in large corporations. SMG should consider collaborative research projects among large businesses, SMEs and universities on a competitive funding basis. These projects would target thematic issues around sustainability and inclusiveness. This could include projects in the field of green entrepreneurship and address environmentally-friendly technologies or projects that improve the situation of disadvantaged segments of society. Various instruments could be employed, such as innovation vouchers which have been tested in a number of countries at national and regional level.

There is also great potential to further exploit opportunities for SME participation in **procurement tendering**. Public procurement should be open and transparent and public-sector vendors should be encouraged to break down work packages into smaller tenders to make them more attractive and available to SMEs. Training in tendering processes and requirements by city officials would help open up more potential for procurement tendering to support social and inclusive SME development.

References

Ahn, S. (2015), "Entry Regulation and Industrial Performance in Korea", presented at 2015 KDI-World Bank International Workshop on Economic Assessment of Regulatory Reform, Korea Development Institute, Sejong.

Bloom, N. and J. Van Reenen, (2007), "Measuring and explaining management practices across firms and countries," *The Quarterly Journal of Economics*, Vol. 122/4, Oxford University Press, Oxford, pp. 1351-1408.

Bravo-Biosca, A., G. Criscuolo and C. Menon (2013), "What Drives the Dynamics of Business Growth?," *OECD Science, Technology and Industry Policy Papers,* No. 1, OECD Publishing, Paris, http://dx.doi.org/10.1787/23074957.

Bruhn, M., D. Karlan and A. Schoar (2010), "What capital is missing in developing countries?", *The American Economic Review*, Vol. 100/2, American Economic Association, Nashville, pp. 629-633.

Chang, W. (2016), "Is Korea's Public Funding for SMEs Achieving Its Intended Goals?", *KDI Focus (February)*, Korea Development Institute, Sejong.

Criscuolo, Gal and C. Menon (2014), "The Dynamics of Employment Growth: New Evidence from 18 Countries", *OECD Science, Technology and Industry Policy Papers,* No. 14, OECD Publishing, Paris, http://dx.doi.org/10.1787/23074957.

Enkel, E., O. Gassmann and H. Chesbrough (2009), "Open R&D and open innovation: exploring the phenomenon," *R&D Management*, Vol. 39/4, Wiley, Hoboken, pp. 311-316.

Hara, H. (2014), "The impact of firm-provided training on productivity, wages, and transition to regular employment for workers in flexible arrangements," *Journal of the Japanese and International Economies*, Vol. 34, Elsevier, Amsterdam, pp. 336-359.

Hlasny, V. (2017), "How Korea's Labor Market Breeds Social Inequality", *The Diplomat*, http://thediplomat.com/2016/11/how-koreas-labor-market-breeds-social-inequality (accessed July 2017).

Interface, website, www.interface-online.org.uk (accessed November 2017).

Kim, J. (2015), "Promoting Good-Quality Job Creation in the Sector of SMEs", *KDI FOCUS*, No. 29, Korea Development Institute, Sejong.

Koske, I., I.Wanner, R. Bitetti and O. Barbiero (2015), "The 2013 Update of the OECD Product Market Regulation Indicators: Policy Insights for OECD and non-OECD countries", *OECD Economics Department Working Papers*, No. 1200, OECD Publishing, Paris, http://dx.doi.org/10.1787/5js3f5d3n2vl-en.

Lee, B. H. and K. Y. Shin (2017), "Job Mobility of Non-Regular Workers in the Segmented Labor Markets: a Cross-national Comparison of South Korea and Japan", *Development and Society*, Vol. 46/1, Institute for Social Development and Policy Research, Seoul.

Mason, C. and R. Brown (2014), "Entrepreneurial ecosystems and growth oriented entrepreneurship", background paper prepared for the workshop organised by the OECD LEED Programme and the Dutch Ministry of Economic Affairs, The Hague, 7 November 2013, www.oecd.org/cfe/leed/entrepreneurial-ecosystems.pdf.

Ministry of Employment and Labour of Korea (2017), Annual survey on working conditions by employment type (database), http://laborstat.molab.go.kr/ (accessed November 2017).

OECD (2017a), *Small, Medium. Strong: Trends in SME Performance and Business Conditions*, OECD Publishing, Paris, http://dx.doi.org/10.1787/9789264275683-en.

OECD (2017b), *Financing SMEs and entrepreneurs 2017: An OECD Scoreboard,* OECD Publishing, Paris, http://dx.doi.org/10.1787/fin_sme_ent-2017-en.

OECD (2017c), *Entrepreneurship at a Glance,* OECD Publishing, Paris, http://dx.doi.org/10.1787/entrepreneur_aag-2017-en.

OECD (2017d), *Boosting Social Enterprise Development : Good Practice Compendium,* OECD Publishing, Paris, http://dx.doi.org/10.1787/9789264268500-en.

OECD (2017e), *OECD Science, Technology and Industry Scoreboard 2017: the digital transformation,* OECD Publishing, Paris, http://dx.doi.org/10.1787/9789264268821-en.

OECD (2017f), *Inclusive Entrepreneurship Compendium,* OECD Publishing, Paris, http://dx.doi.org/10.1787/9789264251496-en.

OECD (2017g), *The Missing Entrepreneurs 2017,* OECD Publishing, Paris, http://dx.doi.org/10.1787/9789264283602-en.

OECD (2016a), *OECD Economic surveys: Korea 2016,* OECD Publishing, Paris, http://dx.doi.org/10.1787/eco_surveys-kor-2016-en.

OECD (2016b), *OECD Employment Outlook 2016*, OECD Publishing, Paris, http://dx.doi.org/10.1787/empl_outlook-2016-en.

OECD (2015a), *The Missing Entrepreneurs 2015,* OECD Publishing, Paris, http://dx.doi.org/10.1787/9789264226418-en.

OECD (2015b), *The Future of Productivity*, OECD Publishing, Paris, http://dx.doi.org/10.1787/9789264248533-en.

OECD (2015c), Product Market Regulation (database), www.oecd.org/economy/pmr (accessed November 2017).

OECD (2007), *OECD Framework for the Evaluation of SME and Entrepreneurship Policies and Programmes,* OECD Publishing, Paris, http://dx.doi.org/10.1787/9789264040090-en.

Roper, S. and N. Hewitt-Dundas (2016), *Market failures in open innovation: implications and policy responses,* Warwick University Enterprise Research Centre, Coventry, https://pure.qub.ac.uk/portal/files/124499231/market_failures_in_open_innovation_imp_and_policy_resp.pdf.

Seoul Metropolitan Government (2017), Background Questionnaire provided to OECD.

Seoul Statistics (database), http://english.seoul.go.kr/get-to-know-us/statistics-of-seoul/seoul-statistics-by-category/ (accessed August 2017).

Whang, U., et al. (2015), "Why did Korean domestic demand slow down after the Asian financial crisis?," *KIEP Policy Analysis*, Korea Institute for International Economic Policy, Sejong.

World Bank (2017), Doing Business in Korea (database), http://www.doingbusiness.org/data/exploreeconomies/korea (Accessed November 2017).

Zahra, S. A. and S. Nambisan (2012), "Entrepreneurship and strategic thinking in business ecosystems," *Business horizons,* Vol.55/3, Elsevier, Amsterdam, pp. 219-229.

ORGANISATION FOR ECONOMIC CO-OPERATION AND DEVELOPMENT

The OECD is a unique forum where governments work together to address the economic, social and environmental challenges of globalisation. The OECD is also at the forefront of efforts to understand and to help governments respond to new developments and concerns, such as corporate governance, the information economy and the challenges of an ageing population. The Organisation provides a setting where governments can compare policy experiences, seek answers to common problems, identify good practice and work to co-ordinate domestic and international policies.

The OECD member countries are: Australia, Austria, Belgium, Canada, Chile, the Czech Republic, Denmark, Estonia, Finland, France, Germany, Greece, Hungary, Iceland, Ireland, Israel, Italy, Japan, Korea, Latvia, Luxembourg, Mexico, the Netherlands, New Zealand, Norway, Poland, Portugal, the Slovak Republic, Slovenia, Spain, Sweden, Switzerland, Turkey, the United Kingdom and the United States. The European Union takes part in the work of the OECD.

OECD Publishing disseminates widely the results of the Organisation's statistics gathering and research on economic, social and environmental issues, as well as the conventions, guidelines and standards agreed by its members.

OECD PUBLISHING, 2, rue André-Pascal, 75775 PARIS CEDEX 16
(84 2018 01 1 P) ISBN 978-92-64-29018-1 – 2018

www.ingramcontent.com/pod-product-compliance
Lightning Source LLC
LaVergne TN
LVHW081411110826
845149LV00010B/1698
9789264290181